NEW DIRECTIONS FOR ADULT AND CONTINUING EDUCATION

Ralph G. Brockett, *University of Tennessee, Knoxville*
EDITOR-IN-CHIEF

Alan B. Knox, *University of Wisconsin, Madison*
CONSULTING EDITOR

Education Through Community Organizations

Michael W. Galbraith
Temple University

EDITOR

Number 47, Fall 1990

JOSSEY-BASS INC., PUBLISHERS
San Francisco

22649497

EDUCATION THROUGH COMMUNITY ORGANIZATIONS
Michael W. Galbraith (ed.)
New Directions for Adult and Continuing Education, no. 47
Ralph G. Brockett, Editor-in-Chief
Alan B. Knox, Consulting Editor

Microfilm copies of issues and articles are available in 16mm and 35mm,
as well as microfiche in 105mm, through University Microfilms Inc., 300
North Zeeb Road, Ann Arbor, Michigan 48106.

LC 85-644750   ISSN 0195-2242   ISBN 1-55542-801-0

NEW DIRECTIONS FOR ADULT AND CONTINUING EDUCATION is part of The
Jossey-Bass Higher and Adult Education Series and is published quarterly
by Jossey-Bass Inc., Publishers (publication number USPS 493-930). Sec-
ond-class postage paid at San Francisco, California, and at additional
mailing offices. Postmaster: Send address changes to Jossey-Bass Inc.,
Publishers, 350 Sansome Street, San Francisco, California 94104.

EDITORIAL CORRESPONDENCE should be sent to the Editor-in-Chief,
Ralph G. Brockett, Dept. of Technological and Adult Education, University
of Tennessee, 402 Claxton Addition, Knoxville, Tennessee 37996-3400.

Cover photograph by Wernher Krutein/PHOTOVAULT © 1990.

Printed on acid-free paper in the United States of America.

CONTENTS

EDITOR'S NOTES

Communities are diverse entities. It is through this diversity that adult learners find educational opportunities to engage in purposeful learning. Adults are continuously involved in a process of developing skills, acquiring knowledge, and reflecting on their experiences. Community members draw on their own powers of creativity and sensitivity to make their learning rewarding. The community provides not only the connection between private and public life but the foundation of our survival as a free and democratic society. In essence, the community becomes the learning environment.

While there are numerous opportunities that contribute to formal, nonformal, and informal adult education, this sourcebook focuses on selected community organizations that use education as an allied function to reach their primary goals. The chapters in this volume are intended to assist adult and continuing educators in recognizing the wide range of educational opportunities that exist in the community and show them how they can help adults find meaning in education through community organizations. A wide range of community organizations are considered here, and the contributors address the key issues: How does providing education assist the organization in reaching its primary goals? Why provide educational opportunities to their clientele and to the community at large? What approaches are employed to enhance learning? Does the organization reach diverse populations such as women, minorities, older adults, the socially isolated, and the educationally disadvantaged? And how do these organizations contribute to the development of self, profession, and community?

To understand the connection between the community and adult education, Chapter One explores the concept of community and examines how the community serves as a context for formal, nonformal, and informal adult education. In Chapter Two, Trenton R. Ferro describes how social and fraternal organizations have discovered that attainment of their mission depends on extensive educational efforts.

In Chapter Three, Burton R. Sisco and Donna L. Whitson suggest that libraries can serve as the people's university in both rural and urban communities. They discuss the Intermountain Community Learning and Information Services project, which responds to the information and educational needs of rural communities through programs and services that are delivered by new technologies as well as traditional methods.

Paulette T. Beatty and Barbara P. Robbins, in Chapter Four, examine how religious institutions serve an educative role in the transformation of the individual, the group, and society itself.

Community-based educational programs that attract older adults are discussed by Brad Courtenay in Chapter Five. Flexibility, he suggests, is the key to success for engaging older learners in educational encounters.

Victoria J. Marsick stresses in Chapter Six that human service organizations have moved toward a philosophy of empowering clients through education. In reaching their goals, however, these organizations find themselves providing learning opportunities for staff as well.

In Chapter Seven, Mary C. Chobot and Richard B. Chobot describe the unique characteristics of museums and explain how they contribute to the education of adults in the community, often with the use of new technology.

Stephen D. Brookfield develops in Chapter Eight a framework for understanding the mass media and recognizing how they can stimulate adults to think critically. He offers two examples of prime-time network television programs that seem to perform a valuable community educational function.

In Chapter Nine, Albert K. Wiswell provides an overview of business and industry activities that contribute to the building of a learning community. He concludes that contributing to the community at large through educational activities is good for business.

David W. Price examines in Chapter Ten how the Cooperative Extension Service develops community education through formal, nonformal, and informal issue-based educational programs.

The final chapter offers a framework for building communities of learners. Drawing on the varied ideas of the previous chapters, it suggests that adult learners, community organizations, and educators must make important choices concerning participation, implementation, and the conduct of education through community organizations.

Michael W. Galbraith
Editor

Michael W. Galbraith is associate professor of adult education and coordinator of graduate studies in adult education at Temple University, Philadelphia. He is a member of several editorial boards for professional journals and is the author of numerous publications including Adult Learning Methods: A Guide for Effective Instruction *(1990),* Facilitating Adult Learning: A Transactional Process *(1990), and* Education in the Rural American Community *(with Paul A. Sundet, in press).*

The community is a natural setting for the adult education process.

The Nature of Community and Adult Education

Michael W. Galbraith

We are all members of some kind of community and we all, whether deliberately or accidentally, participate in some aspect of adult education and learning. Connecting community and adult education is the primary focus of this book. This chapter explores the concept of community and the difficulty of defining the term in simple and definitive terms. It also examines several approaches to studying community and explains how adult education can be a vital component in the community structure. Lastly, it suggests that community is best defined as a natural setting for formal, nonformal, and informal adult education that provides the basis for lifelong education throughout adulthood.

The Concept of Community

Community is multidimensional in scope and perspective. (See Bellah and others, 1985; Effrat, 1974; Galbraith and Sundet, in press; Warren and Lyon, 1988.) The term generates a host of definitions, missions, aims, and images. Community is a value-laden term that evokes a variety of descriptions by a diverse range of individuals.

In reality we live in a mega-community that is international, national, and local in scope. A mega-community is a large-scale systematic community that is connected by cultural, social, psychological, economic, political, environmental, and technological elements. It is a community that can be depicted by its vertical pattern in which each component community and its social relationships are oriented to the international and national society and culture (Warren, 1978). A community may also be depicted by its

NEW DIRECTIONS FOR ADULT AND CONTINUING EDUCATION, no. 47, Fall 1990 © Jossey-Bass Inc., Publishers

horizontal pattern, which is concerned with the relationship of local units to each other. It is through the community's horizontal pattern that the social system performs local and relevant functions, provides education, employment, and income, and establishes a link between various social units and individuals in the community. The horizontal pattern of community assists us in understanding geographic communities as well as how people relate to each other.

Tonnies (1957) used the German terms *gemeinschaft* and *gesellschaft* to describe two ways of how people relate to each other. A *gemeinschaft* community is characteristic of families, neighborhoods, and friendship groups that relate to each other in a sense of mutuality, stability, common identity and concerns, and a common subscription to social norms, bonds, and obligations. A geographic community calls forth an awareness of mutual assistance and development in the interrelationship and cohesiveness of its membership that will ensure a harmonious existence. A *gesellschaft* community is one in which people relate to each other in a means–ends relationship. It is characterized by various forms of exchange with other people for the primary purpose of serving individual interests. There is little sentiment involved, and the rationality within the *gesellschaft* community is definitive in that there is no shared identity, mutuality, or common concern.

Defining Community. Warren (1978, p. 1) suggests that the idea of community is deceptively simple, "so long as one does not ask for a rigid definition." He found through a meta-analysis of some ninety-four definitions of community that sixty-nine definitions included social interaction, common ties, and locational criteria as definitive of the concept. The emphasis on human interaction and relationships within places, as well as common interests, values, and mores, are frequently cited attributes of community. Warren ultimately considered a community to be "that combination of social units and systems which perform the major social functions having locality relevance" (p. 9). This definition suggests that people within the community have local access to a diversity of activities that are necessary in day-to-day living.

While this is considered a geographic definition of community, others suggest that the emphasis should focus on the common interests, concerns, and functions of people. (See Bellah and others, 1985; DeLargy, 1989; Galbraith and Sundet, in press; Hamilton and Cunningham, 1989; Hiemstra, 1972; Newmann and Oliver, 1972; Roberts, 1979; Wright, 1980.) Brookfield (1983) declares that, aside from the familiar locational expression of community, there are "communities of interest" and "communities of function" that may supersede geographic boundaries. Communities of interest are groups of individuals bound by some single common interest or set of common interests such as leisure activities, civic and special political interests, or spiritual and religious beliefs and affiliations. Wright (1980, p. 101) echoes this view by stating that "a community is a collectivity of people differentiated from the total population by a common interest." Communities of function are linked by major life roles such as teacher, attorney, doctor, farmer, student, homemaker, parent, and so forth. As is readily apparent, geographic communities, communities of interest, and communities of function intersect and overlap into the broad conceptualization of community. Another concept of community is derived from the field of educational marketing, which recognizes demographic and psychographic communities. Demographic communities are groups bound by common demographic characteristics such as race, age, and sex. For example, to speak of "the black community" or "the elderly community" is to address a demographic community. Psychographic communities are formed by a commonality of value systems, social class, and life-style, such as "the yuppie community" or "the gay community."

Thus there are numerous frameworks for understanding and defining the word *community*. A community that is characterized by *gemeinschaft* seems most appropriate as it subscribes to a demographic and harmonious existence. From that perspective, I suggest that a community may be defined as the combination of geographic, locational, and nonlocational units, systems, and characteristics that provide relevance and growth to individuals, groups, and organizations.

The Good Community. Warren (1970) coined the phrase "the good community" and pointed to a number of issues embodying it. The issues that follow coincide with what has been described as a *gemeinschaft* community as well as the definition of community just offered. The good community is concerned with primary group relationships, autonomy, viability, power distribution, participation, degree of commitment, degree of heterogeneity, the extent of neighborhood control, and the extent of conflict. Warren suggests that the good community is people-oriented and democratic in nature. It is concerned with the capacity of local people to confront their problems through concerted action, directing themselves to the distribution of power, arranging for participation and commitment in community affairs, understanding how differences among people can be tolerated, and debating the extent of neighborhood control and conflict. Warren's good community suggests that these important issues demand critical reflection, debate, and difficult choices if such a community is to exist.

Newmann and Oliver (1972) echo similar characteristics of a good community. They describe the community as a group in which membership is valued as an end in itself. The community's members share a commitment to stability, subscribe to a set of common social norms, and maintain a sense of shared identity. In addition, the members of a good community have extensive personal contact with each other. Lastly, a community concerns itself with many significant aspects of the members' lives, tolerates competing factions, and has procedures for handling conflict. Kanter (1972,

1974) contends that the search for the good community is a quest for direction and purpose in the collective anchoring of the individual life.

While these authors have addressed the good community and its characteristics from a local perspective, they say much to us about the challenge of developing the good mega-community that affects the international and national dimensions of our lives.

Studying the Community. If we are to understand the concept of community, a brief description of the approaches to studying the community should be included. The diverse approaches that can be used, as well as their contributions, can assist us in recognizing the complexity of the concept of community and how adult education can be a vital component in the community structure. One approach is to study the community as a network of spatial relationships (Warren, 1978). In this approach we investigate people and institutions and their distribution throughout geographical space—for example, rural or urban communities. Another approach is to study the community as people—that is, to define the character of the community by the kinds of people who live there. In this type of study, a careful analysis is made of the kinds of people who reside in the community, the various age groups, racial and nationality groups, sex, mobility, and the rates of change over a period of time.

Apart from the approaches of space and population, the community can be investigated according to the notion of shared institutions and values. This approach suggests that certain institutions and values are held in common by the local population. Warren (1978) suggests that "the shared institutional services are thought to constitute a shared way of life . . . and that the function of making accessible locally the various institutional facilities for daily living needs is, from the ecological standpoint, the chief reason for existence of the community" (p. 34). He continues by arguing that shared values "are thought of not only as a basic component of what is meant by the community, but also as an important item on which communities often differ greatly from each other" (p. 34). A fourth approach to studying the community is through the interactions of local people and their association with one another, their behavior with regard to one another, and such major institutions as the family, the church, government, and education. Points of departure arise through social processes such as conflict, competition, disorganization, dissociation, and the degree and dimensions of community action.

The final two approaches involve studying the community as a distribution of power and as a social system (Rothman and Tropman, 1987; Suttles, 1972; Warren, 1978). Power is concerned with how social behavior is influenced—by individuals or by formal or informal organizations in the community. This approach focuses on power structures and the consequences of policy decisions on the lives of individuals, groups, and organizations within the community. The social system concept, by contrast, is based on the idea of "structured interaction between two or more units" (Warren, 1978, p. 46). It is concerned with how the various structures of the interaction endure through time. Warren contends that to study the community one must recognize that it is a system of systems, that it is not structurally and functionally centralized in the same sense as a formal organization, and that as a social system it is implicit in nature as compared with the explicitness of a formal organization (pp. 48–49).

It has been suggested that the concept of community is multidimensional in scope, both in practice and in theory. The concept of adult education is also multidimensional in that it utilizes formal, nonformal, and informal mechanisms to bring about individual, group, and community change. The connection between community and adult education seems to be a natural process. Conceptualizing the community and adult education helps us to understand the connection they both have to society at large.

Connecting Community and Adult Education

The concepts of community and adult education have historically been connected (Knowles, 1977) and remain a major focus in understanding adult education as a discipline and field of practice. (See Boone and Associates, 1980; Boyd, Apps, and Associates, 1980; Brookfield, 1983; Merriam and Cunningham, 1989; Roberts, 1979.) In the Handbook of Adult and Continuing Education (Merriam and Cunningham, 1989), the majority of chapters are dedicated to understanding adult education as a field of practice, the adult educational process, providers of educational programs, program areas, and special clienteles. Each operates in some framework of community, whether from a locational or nonlocational perspective (communities of interest and communities of function). It is through these nonlocational features that formal, nonformal, and informal adult learning is facilitated and by which most adult education programs are designed.

Courtney (1989, p. 24) defines adult education as the "intervention into the ordinary business of life—an intervention whose immediate goal is change, in knowledge or in competence." From his definition it can be assumed that adult education is an intervening process that effects change in individuals, groups, and locational and nonlocational communities who comprise a larger community context. Within this scope of inquiry, adult education has the potential to affect the way that individuals, groups, and communities live, inform, and educate themselves. Adult education can serve as a means for self-fulfillment as well as for social, political, and psychological empowerment. When community and adult education are connected both conceptually and in practice, a unique relationship is developed that offers communities and individuals a sense of hope and dignity, a sense of responsibility for their own communities and lives, and a voice in the social and political arenas. The connection suggests a liberating significance for individuals, groups, and communities.

A connection between community and adult education was made by Boyd and Apps (1980) in a three-dimensional model for understanding adult education that includes transactional modes, client focus, and personal, social, and cultural systems. Each dimension has three aspects: individual, group, and community. Their conceptual model emphasizes the nature of the learner's situation, the benefits of the educational activity, and how personal, cultural, and social systems are configured in terms of values, norms, beliefs, characteristics, and so forth. While they suggest that community is one aspect of each dimension, in reality the multidimensional aspects of community are in each of the three aspects: individual, group, and community.

In another study, Brookfield (1983) focused on the community context of adult education. He suggests that the neighborhood notion (the locational concept) of community is most appropriate to adult education, and he connects community and adult education through a typology consisting of adult education *for* the community, adult education *in* the community, and adult education *of* the community. Within his typology "adult education practices can display a greater or lesser awareness of the structure and concerns of the community in which they are located" (p. 84). Basically he focuses on the role of the educator, the dimensions of learner control, and the value base underlying community and adult education.

As evidenced by the authors cited above, there are many ways of conceptualizing the community and adult education. Another way of discussing the connection between community and adult education is by viewing the community as a context for formal, nonformal, and informal adult education. From this perspective, the agencies, organizations, and activities in the community are connected with the field of adult education. This approach suggests how adult education can serve as an intervention in bringing about change and growth for adult learners, groups, and communities as well as the roles played by adult educators.

Community as Context for Formal Adult Education. This category consists of for-profit and nonprofit organizations in the community who have as their primary function the delivery of formal education in which adult learners may participate. In most cases the goal of the adult learner is to acquire some type of credential, certificate, or degree. Providers in this category would include state and regional universities and colleges, community colleges, proprietary schools, vocational and technical institutes, external degree agencies, and public adult education schools. Educators are likely to be experts in some other field and probably do not consider themselves professional adult educators. Learners in such settings have little control over what is taught and how it is taught. Educators make value judgments of what is appropriate, desirable, and realistic for learners to acquire through their formal educational pursuits.

Community as Context for Nonformal Adult Education. Communities are comprised of a number of organizations that use education as a secondary function of their mission. Adult learners who participate in nonformal adult education are motivated by the desire to learn the activity that is presented. Community organizations such as cooperative extension, religious institutions, health institutions, service clubs, voluntary organizations, business and industry human resources development programs, correctional institutions, libraries, museums, senior citizen organizations, and a host of other community-based agencies are examples of such providers of nonformal adult education. In these settings adult learners are more likely to participate voluntarily and are not specifically seeking credentials or degrees, though they may receive a certificate of completion. Through these organizations adult learners retain some control over their learning needs as well as when, how, and where these needs can be satisfied. Educators in community nonformal adult education operate on a nonstructured to structured continuum. They may or may not be trained in teaching adults but nevertheless seem to be quite successful.

Community as Context for Informal Adult Education. This category consists of the vast majority of adult education that takes place within the community. It is independent of institutions and organizations. The community itself is the instrument of education, and adult learners are guided by their own desires and learning processes. Learning in this context may be deliberate or fortuitous, but it is always personally meaningful to the adult learner. Informal adult education is characterized by interaction between human and nonhuman resources: informal debates and conversations in the work, family, or community setting, television and other mass media viewing, travel, recreational activities, and listening to audio cassettes, reading publications, or viewing videotapes. The adult learner has complete control over what the learning will comprise and how and where it will occur. Although the adult learner may consult with others concerning the learning project, in most cases there is no professionally trained educator. The community serves as the educator in conjunction with serving as a learning resource and laboratory.

Community, Adult Education, and Lifelong Education

It has been suggested that both the community and adult education are multidimensional in scope and perspective. Connecting community and adult education should stimulate and contribute to the lifelong education process.

The ultimate goal of any community should be to develop a democratic and educated citizenry. As Lindeman (1926) observed: "The whole of life is learning, therefore education can have no endings" (p. 6). Lifelong learning is realized through the community and its educational processes. Adult education can contribute to the development of a lifelong education community consisting of individuals, groups, and communities of interest and function. It must be recognized, though, that adult education and lifelong education are not synonymous. The process of adult education can only address the adulthood dimension of lifelong education. The concept of lifelong education suggests that it occurs throughout the entire life span (the vertical dimension) and that education and life are linked (the horizontal dimension). The community and formal, nonformal, and informal adult education are the context in which adult learners recognize their identity, potential, and significance within the lifelong education process. It is a way of creating the good community that exercises and demonstrates the elements of a harmonious existence.

References

Bellah, R., Madsen, R., Sullivan, W., Swidler, A., and Tipton, S. *Habits of the Heart: Individualism and Commitment in American Life.* New York: Harper & Row, 1985.

Boone, E., Shearon, R., White, E., and Associates. *Serving Personal and Community Needs Through the Community.* San Francisco: Jossey-Bass, 1980.

Boyd, R., and Apps, J. "A Conceptual Model for Adult Education." In R. Boyd, J. Apps, and Associates, *Redefining the Discipline of Adult Education.* San Francisco: Jossey-Bass, 1980.

Boyd, R., Apps, J., and Associates. *Redefining the Discipline of Adult Education.* San Francisco: Jossey-Bass, 1980.

Brookfield, S. *Adult Learners, Adult Education and the Community.* New York: Teachers College Press, 1983.

Courtney, S. "Defining Adult and Continuing Education." In S. Merriam and P. Cunningham (eds.), *Handbook of Adult and Continuing Education.* San Francisco: Jossey-Bass, 1989.

DeLargy, P. "Public Schools and Community Education." In S. Merriam and P. Cunningham (eds.), *Handbook of Adult and Continuing Education.* San Francisco: Jossey-Bass, 1989.

Effrat, M. (ed.). *The Community: Approaches and Applications.* New York: Free Press, 1974.

Galbraith, M. W., and Sundet, P. A. (eds.). *Education in the Rural American Community: A Lifelong Process.* Malabar, Fla.: Krieger, in press.

Hamilton, E., and Cunningham, P. "Community-Based Adult Education." In S. Merriam and P. Cunningham (eds.), *Handbook of Adult and Continuing Education.* San Francisco: Jossey-Bass, 1989.

Hiemstra, R. *The Educative Community.* Lincoln, Nebr.: Professional Educators Publications, 1972.

Kanter, R. *Commitment and Community: Communes and Utopias in Sociological Perspective.* Cambridge, Mass.: Harvard University Press, 1972.

Kanter, R. "Utopian Communities." In M. Effrat (ed.), *The Community: Approaches and Applications.* New York: Free Press, 1974.

Knowles, M. *The Adult Education Movement in the United States.* Malabar, Fla.: Krieger, 1977.

Lindeman, E. *The Meaning of Adult Education.* New York: New Republic, 1926.

Merriam, S., and Cunningham, P. (eds.). *Handbook of Adult and Continuing Education.* San Francisco: Jossey-Bass, 1989.

Newmann, F., and Oliver, D. "Education and Community." In D. Purpel and M. Belanger (eds.), *Curriculum and the Cultural Revolution.* Berkeley, Calif.: McCutchan, 1972.

Roberts, H. *Community Development: Learning and Action.* Toronto: University of Toronto Press, 1979.

Rothman, J., and Tropman, J. "Models of Community Organization and Macro Practice Perspectives: Their Mixing and Phasing." In F. Cox, J. Erlich, J. Rothman, and J. Tropman (eds.), *Strategies of Community Organization.* Itasca, Ill.: Peacock, 1987.

Suttles, G. *The Social Construction of Communities.* Chicago: University of Chicago Press, 1972.

Tonnies, F. *Community and Society.* East Lansing: Michigan State University Press, 1957.

Warren, R. "The Good Community—What Would It Be?" *Journal of the Community Development Society,* 1970, *1* (1), 14–23.

Warren, R. *The Community in America.* (3rd ed.) Chicago: Rand McNally, 1978.

Warren, R., and Lyon, L. (eds.). *New Perspectives on the American Community.* (5th ed.) Chicago: Dorsey, 1988.

Wright, J. "Community Learning: A Frontier for Adult Education." In R. Boyd, J. Apps, and Associates, *Redefining the Discipline of Adult Education.* San Francisco: Jossey-Bass, 1980.

Michael W. Galbraith is associate professor of adult education and coordinator of graduate studies in adult education at Temple University, Philadelphia.

While social and fraternal organizations with voluntary membership have been established to further diverse missions, they have discovered that the attainment of their organizational objectives depends on extensive educational efforts.

Social and Fraternal Organizations as Educators

Trenton R. Ferro

More than 150 years ago Alexis de Tocqueville noted that America is a nation of joiners: "Americans of all ages, all conditions, and all dispositions, constantly form associations. . . . Wherever, at the head of some new undertaking, you see the Government in France, or a man of rank in England, in the United States you will be sure to find an association" (1947, p. 319). This proclivity to form associations has resulted in a host of voluntary social and fraternal organizations—groups one joins by choice because of special interest in the purposes, goals, and activities of the organizations and because of the opportunities these groups provide people in meeting their personal needs.

In order to accomplish their mission and goals, these groups are consistently involved in the development and promotion of educational endeavors. This chapter provides an overview of these pursuits. Although tremendous diversity exists among the educational aspects and features of social and fraternal organizations, these educational efforts will be presented, for purposes of organization and clarity, around several basic themes together with illustrations drawn from specific organizations. (The comments quoted in the following pages are taken from the responses to my request for information originally sent to some thirty-five national and international organizations.) Readers desiring to learn more about these or other groups should consult the *Encyclopedia of Associations: 1990* (Burek, Kock, and Novallo, 1989) for addresses, phone numbers, contact persons, and other information.

Perceived Role or Function of Education

If anything characterizes the educational efforts of volunteer organizations, it is diversity. This characteristic begins at the top, with mission and goals,

NEW DIRECTIONS FOR ADULT AND CONTINUING EDUCATION, no. 47, Fall 1990 © Jossey-Bass Inc., Publishers

and is exemplified in numerous ways. Sometimes the term *education* is actually included in an organization's statement of mission: "The purpose of The National Exchange Club is to educate, improve, and/or develop the capabilities of the members . . . and of the citizens of the communities, municipalities, and states in which . . . clubs are chartered." Or to cite another example: "The objects of [Veterans of Foreign Wars of the United States] are fraternal, patriotic, historical and educational."

More frequently the stated goals of social and fraternal organizations include no mention of education. Nevertheless, the prominence that some organizations give education is seen in their assigning to a board or committee the responsibility of developing and carrying out educational activities. For example, the national structure of the General Federation of Women's Clubs (GFWC) includes three divisions (continuing education, leadership, and school issues) in its Education Department. The National Association for the Advancement of Colored People's Committee on Education is charged with extensive responsibilities to seek out and attempt to eradicate racial prejudice in schools, to attain racial balance in staffing and school board membership, and to foster high standards of participation and achievement by students. The Soroptimist International accomplishes its community service goals through six program and service areas, one of which is education.

Even though no mention is made in their mission statement and no specific board or department exists, educational efforts and pursuits still pervade the activities of many organizations. The Junior Chamber International (JCI) and the United States Jaycees conduct extensive leadership training and personal development programs; the efforts of Kiwanis International include training of volunteer leadership, leadership skills development, general membership education, community awareness programs, and youth education; and the National Urban League, through its National Education Initiative, has established as a "priority program area . . . a program to improve the achievement of African American public school students." In still other cases groups pursue educational goals to the extent that they either directly or through the establishment of special foundations provide scholarship funds and other support so that both general and specified populations might engage in advanced and continuing education and training—for example, the National Association of American Business Clubs (AMBUCS), Elks, Lions, Pilot Club International, and Rotary International.

Purpose and Focus of Educational Ventures

The efforts of social and fraternal organizations to attain their educational goals, whether stated or implicit, fall generally into five categories. First, the purpose cited by the greatest number is leadership training and personal development opportunities provided for, and experienced by, members as they carry out service projects and fill leadership positions in the organization (GFWC, Optimists, Ruritan National, Soroptimists). Certain groups, such as JCI, Kiwanis, and the U.S. Jaycees, have developed extensive, widely recognized, award-winning programs that utilize leaders trained in the best theory and practice in adult development and learning.

Second, and possibly the most visible, are those programs in which the associations serve as funding sources by providing grants, scholarships, awards, and other forms of assistance both to special projects and to persons pursuing educational and training goals. Often this support reflects national service goals and activities. For example, the National Association of American Business Clubs' "Scholarships for Therapists" program supports the training of professionals for work with the handicapped; the Lions offer vocational training as part of their service to the blind; the Pilot International Foundation (PIF) provides grants to local projects designed to help the disabled as well as scholarships to persons seeking second careers or wishing to extend their education in fields relating to disabled citizens, as well as to persons desiring to enter such careers; and the Soroptimist International's Women's Development Project in Peru "helps women in the Peruvian highlands through a holistic education program teaching health practices and income-producing skills." More familiar are scholarship programs supported by such organizations as the Elks, NAACP, and Ruritan that afford high school students the opportunity to pursue postsecondary degrees. Certain scholarship programs reflect the changing social climate: The Elks provide, through their Vocational Grant Program, two years of technical training for dislocated workers, and the Soroptimists offer grants "to mature women for education/training or retraining to enable them to upgrade their job status or re-enter the work force." Rotary International's educational grant and scholarship programs emphasize the promotion of international awareness and understanding.

Third, there is a wide-ranging group of programs that might be categorized under the label of community and public education, awareness, and service. Most social, civic, and fraternal organizations are involved in a host of local programs that often include educational components and goals (expressly so stated by, for example, Kiwanis, Ruritan, and Soroptimists). These frequently take the form of attempts to make the public more cognizant of some specific activity, problem, or area of concern. Public education and awareness programs sponsored by national organizations also receive their major support at the local level; the Elks' Drug Awareness Program, Lions' Lion-Quest (drug awareness) and "Don't Be Blind to Diabetes" efforts, and the Optimists' "Just Say No" and "Respect for Law" programs are illustrative.

Fourth, there are programs of advocacy that attempt to influence public attitudes and policy. The NAACP, through its Education Committee, monitors public policy and seeks to educate the general populace concerning racial prejudice and unfair school practices. Recognizing "the crucially important role of education in social and economic advancement," the NAACP is concerned about the appropriate preparation of teachers, and its major efforts are directed toward fostering equality in traditional education (through, for instance, its Afro-Academic, Cultural, Technological and Scientific Olympics and its support of Elderhostel). All of the National Urban League's 113 affiliates have responded to its National Education Initiative by planning and developing a wide-ranging and far-reaching set of efforts designed "to work with schools and to make them more effective for African American students." Soroptimist International's support of literacy awareness (Krey, 1989) and the Women's Development Project in Peru reflects its concern "with effecting change at the national and international level to improve the quality of life for people throughout the world."

Fifth, practically all groups are involved in efforts that can best be described as diverse, diffuse, or general in nature and orientation. Among the purposes of the General Federation of Women's Clubs are "promoting all aspects of education to bring about a more literate society" and "taking an active role in leadership for the preservation of our country's resources." The National Exchange Club (NEC) lists, as a benefit of membership, the "exchange of ideas"; Soroptimist International cites "education and heightened awareness"; and the VFW mentions insights gained from participation in its annual Legislative Conference and National Convention. On the basis of this overview, one could draw the conclusion that every effort carried out by social and fraternal organizations has educative potential.

Responsibility for Educational Programming

Here, as much as anywhere, is demonstrated the unique nature of the American social and fraternal organization. Invariably, educational efforts at the local level are conducted by volunteer members of the local chapter. Volunteer participation as educational leaders is also the norm at the regional and even national levels. An exception to this is the U.S. Jaycees, who develop certified trainers to conduct their leadership training and personal development courses. Even when staff members are responsible for the educational programs of the organization (JCI, Kiwanis, Ruritan, U.S. Jaycees), they are often carrying out the policies, plans, and programs established by a volunteer board or committee (NAACP, Ruritan). It should be noted that it is not always easy to determine who is responsible for planning educational programs and carrying out educational functions; such persons are seldom mentioned in the materials supplied by the various associations. For instance, the federation education adviser who wrote an article in *The Soroptimist of the Americas* (Krey, 1989) is not referenced elsewhere in the materials I received.

Furthermore, responsibility at the national level for a club's educational programs is often one of several responsibilities of a staff member, usually the executive secretary or director (Ruritan). Only rarely is there a person designated solely for educational and training functions (JCI), and even more rarely does that person come to that position with an educational background and experience in such areas as adult, community, or continuing education or human resource development (Kiwanis, U.S. Jaycees). In addition, national and organization members often work in cooperation with professional trainers and companies at JCI, while the National Urban League commands "the only national network of human service professionals that can—from an advocacy position—identify key education issues facing the African American community."

Designated Audiences

Above all, the educational efforts of many social and fraternal organizations are designed for the benefit of their own membership; such a benefit is often a key reason why a person affiliates with a particular group. The general public is also the beneficiary of various community awareness programs planned at the local level (Kiwanis) as well as ongoing national programs—such as combatting illiteracy (Rotary), drug abuse awareness (Elks, Optimists, Rotary), respect for the law (Optimists), concern for the aging (Rotary), public education related to blindness and diabetes (Lions), and concerns related to racial prejudice, equality, and integration (NAACP, National Urban League). Although its Individual Development and Personal Growth programs are designed for members, the U.S. Jaycees often make these offerings available to the public through state Jaycee organizations in what are known as ID Colleges. A third group of beneficiaries are the recipients of the various grants and scholarships offered by various organizations (AMBUCS, Elks, Lions, NAACP, Pilot, Rotary, Ruritan, Soroptimists).

Both regular and special programs of social and fraternal organizations benefit explicitly designated populations. The Lions provide direct services to the blind, including sheltered workshops for blind workers and vocational training that enables others to join the regular work force. The Elks and Optimists have geared their drug abuse and drug awareness campaigns directly to at-risk youth, while Pilot International's efforts aid the handicapped and those who work with them. AMBUCS also benefits the handicapped through its "Scholarships for Therapists" program. The NAACP and the National Urban League serve the black community both directly and through their intervention and advocacy efforts with government, business, and industry.

Methods and Techniques

There are, first of all, the standard formats of education and communication used by almost every organization—magazines, newsletters, conferences, and conventions. Some of these are designed deliberately to be educational vehicles or to include items related somehow to education (Soroptimist International). In other instances, educational activities are more incidental but still present (VFW). Social and fraternal organizations use a wide range of delivery methods to achieve their stated objectives: scholarships and grants (AMBUCS, Elks, Lions, NAACP, Pilot International, Rotary, Ruritan, Soroptimists); sponsorship of service clubs for high school and college youth (Kiwanis, Optimists, Pilot International); community action (NAACP, National Urban League); school-based programs and assemblies (Lions, Optimists); marches and rallies (Optimists); and awards and recognitions (Optimists, Soroptimists).

When the development of members is the primary objective, methods and materials reflect customary adult education practices. Manuals, workshops, seminars, and the use of experience both as a knowledge base and as a method of learning are all present. For example, JCI produces its own management and training manuals, *One Year to Lead* and *Vanguard Leaders;* it conducts seminars for small-business owners; its Training for Trainers Program (TROT) equips members to design and present effective training programs, and its course offerings include marketing, mind mapping, body language, telephone skills, burnout, interview techniques, communication skills, speed reading, creative planning, professional presentations, leadership skills, motivation, negotiating techniques, stress management, and time management. Through its Certified Trainers Program the U.S. Jaycees develop workshop leaders at four levels—graduate, associate member, member, and fellow. These trainers have available to them an extensive manual that outlines adult learning characteristics, methods, and techniques. Furthermore, the U.S. Jaycees also produce individual development handbooks on speaking, leadership, writing, management, social skills, family skills, and career skills. Kiwanis' Leadership Development Program is based on adult education principles formulated in specific behavioral objectives and delivered using a broad combination of experiential and participative techniques. The Lions provide films, discussion guides, posters, and informative brochures in support of their public awareness efforts, and Ruritan develops materials and outlines for local training and collaborates in the conduct of workshops on developing community leadership.

Other Special Characteristics

In the process of preparing this chapter, I found that certain aspects of the educational efforts of social and fraternal organizations did not fit into the previous classification categories but are nonetheless worthy of mention. For example, the programs of JCI and the Soroptimists, unlike the others surveyed, are international in perspective and emphasis. The General Federation of Women's Clubs states that it "is responsible for the establishment of 75 percent of America's public libraries"; it also maintains the Women's History and Resource Center and Library, which is not only open to its membership but is also available for scholarly investigations. The Kiwanis claim that one of their competitors "observed our Leadership Development Program and stated that we are at least ten years ahead of other service organizations," while the Optimists highlight the direct involvement of their members with youth, often on a one-to-one basis. Finally, the efforts of the U.S. Jaycees to use adult education principles is evident when they encourage members to participate only in seminars conducted by certified trainers, an effort underscored by offering continuing-education credits to those attending such programs.

Conclusion

The function of education in social and fraternal organizations is certainly diverse, ranging from deliberate, specific, and concerted educational endeavors to informal—one might even be tempted to say incidental—learning activities. Just as varied are the goals underlying these activities. This concluding section presents a taxonomy of the educational objectives of social and fraternal organizations drawn from the preceding discussion. These associations undertake educational efforts to:

- Inform the public about special concerns pertinent to their organizational members (NAACP, National Urban League, VFW)
- Improve the lot of those members represented by the organization (NAACP, National Urban League, VFW)
- Inform, educate, and support specific populations who are not members (AMBUCS, Elks, Kiwanis, Lions, Optimists, Pilot, Rotary, Soroptimists)
- Inform and educate the public about specific populations who are not members (Elks, Kiwanis, Lions, NAACP, National Urban League, Optimists, Rotary, Soroptimists)
- Offer educational opportunities to the general public (GFWC, JCI)
- Provide their own membership both with general education and with training to function as members and leaders in meeting the goals of the organization (GFWC, JCI, Kiwanis, NEC, Optimists, Ruritan, Soroptimists, U.S. Jaycees, VFW)
- Train members to be leaders outside the organization (JCI, U.S. Jaycees)
- Prepare members to become educational facilitators (JCI, U.S. Jaycees)
- Provide scholarship assistance so that others can pursue their educational goals (AMBUCS, Elks, NAACP, Ruritan, Soroptimists)
- Provide scholarship assistance for others so that the organization's goals might be met (AMBUCS, Lions, Pilot, Rotary)
- Carry out general educational goals without specifying content or audience (GFWC, NEC, Soroptimists, VFW).

What is the common thread that runs through all this diversity? Possibly the most striking characteristic is potential impact—the full range of educational endeavors supported by social and fraternal organizations is capable of reaching an extremely wide and varied audience. Prospective beneficiaries include all citizens, regardless of age, geographic location, race, or ability. As a result, many in this land may be involved in lifelong learning even though they do not realize, and might even deny, that they are participating in educational pursuits. Such is the nature of voluntary associations and their programs.

References

Burek, D. M., Kock, K. E., and Novallo, A. (eds.). *Encyclopedia of Associations: 1990.* (24th ed.) Detroit, Mich.: Gale Research, 1989.
de Tocqueville, A. *Democracy in America.* (H. Reeve, trans.; H. S. Commager, ed.) New York: Oxford University Press, 1947. (Originally published 1835 and 1840.)
Krey, I. "Literacy: A Prime Objective." *Soroptimist of the Americas,* 1989, 62 (4), 4-6.

Trenton R. Ferro, assistant professor in adult and community education at Indiana University of Pennsylvania, has had twenty-five years of experience as a professional in volunteer associations and not-for-profit organizations.

Outside of formal educational settings one of the strongest links between learning opportunities and adults in the community is the library.

Libraries: The People's University

Burton R. Sisco, Donna L. Whitson

Libraries as universities of the people have been an enduring part of the adult education tradition in the United States. Beginning in colonial times and continuing through the present, libraries have provided an important educative function in the promotion of an educated citizenry. The link between adults in the community and the library for learning opportunities is inescapable. As André Maurois (1961) wrote concerning the role of the public library: "Nothing, then, is more important for mankind than to bring within the reach of all these means of broadening our horizons, escaping from ourselves and making discoveries which literally transform life and make an individual a more valuable member of society. And the only way to do this is through public libraries" (pp. 169–170). Although Alvin Johnson (1938) described the library as the "people's university," this idea was not new and continues to be debated today. Just how the libraries, especially public libraries, fulfill their function and contribute to the educational needs of adults is the focus of this chapter.

The relationship between adult educators and librarians has fluctuated over the years but has never been severed. In fact the early development of the American Library Association (ALA) and the American Association for Adult Education (AAAE) paralleled each other (Knowles, 1977). In light of the current information age and the exponential explosion of information, never has it been more critical to take stock of how both groups can work together to serve the lifelong needs of society. To understand where we are today, we need to look at where we have been and how we got there.

Historical Development

Early libraries in this country were not publicly accessible, as most were privately owned collections. Many of the major institutions of higher edu-

NEW DIRECTIONS FOR ADULT AND CONTINUING EDUCATION, no. 47, Fall 1990 © Jossey-Bass Inc., Publishers

cation began with private collections donated as part of their establishment. Among those were Harvard in 1638, Yale in 1717, and Kings College (which later became Columbia University) in 1757. These libraries were used by a privileged few. Shera (1949) noted that a second influence on the development of early American libraries was the church. An Anglican clergyman, Reverend Thomas Bray, was instrumental in the establishment of thirty-nine parish libraries along the Atlantic coast at the beginning of the eighteenth century. As a representative of the Society for Promoting Christian Knowledge, he wanted American clergy to have access to book resources. Again the public did not routinely have access to these collections.

In 1731, with the advent of Benjamin Franklin's Junto, a wider range of the population had book collections made available to them. Because the Junto was established for intellectual improvement and social enjoyment, members needed resources to stimulate their discussions. The private collections of members were pooled into one consolidated collection to support the Junto. This collection became the Library Company of Philadelphia and has been called "the mother of all subscription libraries in North America" (Rose, 1954, p. 15). Although these libraries served more of the population, only those with the means to pay could use the collection. These early subscription libraries existed in several forms and included association, society, mercantile, and social libraries, depending on the establishing group.

Similar libraries continued to grow and expand without much change until the middle of the nineteenth century. In 1833 citizens of Peterborough, New Hampshire, voted for a portion of tax money to be used for the purchase of books and the first American town library was opened to the public. The action set a precedent for library use of public funds, and other free libraries began to appear. The Mechanics and Lyceum movements that became prominent in the 1830–1850 period promoted the growth of these libraries (Knowles, 1977). The public library concept was firmly established in the Boston Public Library in 1852 with the idea of "providing equal educational opportunities for adults" (Lee, 1966, p. 9). While the subscription libraries served members' specific needs, the new public libraries promoted the concepts of a yet-to-be-defined discipline of adult education. Although the primary users of these libraries tended to be scholarly types, the public library movement continued to expand. Until the turn of the century, library educational services focused on personal development, moral improvement, and civic enlightenment.

As the twentieth century approached, a growing industrial society in America saw a change from rural to urban population centers. The nation's concerns were changing also. Public libraries "became one of the centers where a new social consciousness was born" (Rose, 1954, p. 26). Libraries expanded to serve larger portions of the population. A major influence on library development in this era was Andrew Carnegie, who provided $41 million for library construction: "My reasons for selecting public libraries being my belief, as Carlyle has recorded, that the true university of these days is a collection of books, and that thus such libraries are entitled to a first place as instruments for the elevation of the masses of the people" (Learned, 1924, p. 70).

In the 1920s and 1930s the real action between libraries and adult education began. In 1924 the American Library Association (ALA) appointed a commission on library and adult education. As a part of the Carnegie-backed investigation, under the direction of President Frederick Keppel, to determine the need for a national adult education association, the ALA commission studied the role of the library in adult education. The commission issued a series of bulletins called *Adult Education and the Library*, among whose contributors were Morse Cartwright, Frederick Keppel, and Everett Dean Martin. William Learned's (1924) view of the library as a dynamic intelligence center of the community was ignored in the studies, and the commission presented a limited peripheral role for libraries in adult education. Readers' advisory services and discussion group support became the major activities supporting adult education. These activities helped interested library users and librarians to develop a linkage in the effort to locate particular materials, book materials, and assigned readings.

In the 1940s and 1950s individual and group service support continued. Public library objectives adopted in 1956 included facilitating informal self-education. In 1957 the American Library Association established the Adult Education Division (renamed the Adult Services Division) to further the educational, cultural, and recreational development of the adult population. In the 1950s and 1960s federal and formulation funding led to the enhancement of library services to adults. In the 1970s and 1980s libraries began to re-examine their roles in adult education. The independent learning project experiments of the 1970s were reflected in public library service such as serving as an educational brokering service that linked library users and community providers as well as assistance for self-directed learning activities. In the 1980s literacy programs were incorporated into many public libraries (Smith, 1990). Adult education activities are supported in theory, but in practice, especially in small rural libraries, the recreational reading aspect and children's programming tend to take precedence over educational activities. Only now is the pendulum beginning to swing in the other direction. The future depends on proactive visionary leadership from the library and adult education communities.

Libraries and Their Mission

Although there is a commonly held perception that libraries are libraries, there are four basic types of libraries with very different missions. School libraries serve public and private students by supporting the K-12 curriculum. Obviously there are no real connections with adult education from these libraries. The remaining three types—academic, special, and public—do have various connections to adult education.

Academic libraries see their role as supporting the teaching, research, and service missions of their respective institutions of higher education. Few formal adult education services are offered by most academic libraries other than support for self-directed learners. Recently some academic libraries have recognized the influx of adult nontraditional students into higher education, and some are providing special services and assistance (Smith, 1990).

Special libraries include company libraries for business and industry, medical libraries, agency libraries, and a host of others serving specialized clientele. They primarily provide information support more than formalized adult education activities.

Public libraries have provided information support and conducted formal adult education programming from their inception. Throughout their existence they have worked as partners with adult educators in a variety of ways.

Public Library Service to Adults

The four continuing roles of the public library as defined by the ALA include (1) a nontraditional educational agency mediating between the total record of human experience and the individual, (2) a cultural agency fostering creativity, enjoyment of literature and the arts, and appreciation for America's pluralistic culture, (3) an information agency providing a bridge between the individual and community resources and between the multiplicity of disciplines within the record, as well as keys to the wisdom in the record, and (4) a rehabilitation agency helping to bring the handicapped and deviant into their full potential (Maurois, 1961; Smith, 1990).

Public libraries more than any other library have responded to user needs and desires for service. These services include many informal adult education activities. Public libraries sponsor a variety of cultural activities from art exhibits to film festivals. Adult programming includes formal and informal classes ranging from frivolous to serious that are often carried out jointly with other community educational agencies. In response to the growing interest in computer literacy, recently libraries have provided public-access computers and offered seminars in word processing and spreadsheet usage. Parenting classes are often held while preschoolers are involved in story hour programs in the library. Helping adults make community connections to a variety of agencies, individuals, and programs is accomplished by the maintenance of an information and referral file. In one form or another, reader's advisory services or independent learner assistance are available in many libraries, mostly in urban settings. Vocational counseling, guidance, and referral services are fast-growing programs of recent years. The ALA's Public Library Division now has a section titled Adult Lifelong Learning that even has a subcommittee on job and career information services (Smith, 1990).

As public libraries continue to evaluate their role as information provider, stronger programs are being developed to ensure access to information through networking with other types of libraries and information providers. Technology is one of the chief components in facilitating this process.

Studies have shown that clients' information/education needs are very similar in both rural and urban settings, but availability and access differ greatly in the two contexts (McDaniel, 1986, p. 2). Some of the barriers cited by rural learners are distance, travel, geographic isolation, and limited access to educational opportunities including resources and facilities. Rural adults often say they suffer more from economic decline yet have to pay more for education than their urban counterparts. The challenge of meeting these needs is being addressed in a number of innovative ways. Some libraries offer a "books-by-mail" service that provides a printed catalogue of titles which can be ordered by patrons living too far from a library. Selected titles are often sent along with postage-paid return envelopes. In addition, some libraries offer bookmobile programs that serve the homebound and sight and hearing impaired, particularly the elderly. In some areas county libraries are making closer connections with their rural branches by install-ing toll-free telephone lines and providing FAX machines. Computer net-works with data bases containing the holdings of other state, regional, and national libraries are being made available to rural areas also. Yet another re-evaluation of the library's role in adult education has been prompted by all these rapidly emerging technologies. On-line computer catalogues, on-line data-base searching, electronic mail, and FAX machines are but a few of the technological advances affecting library services. More and more libraries are assuming a brokering role as a link between users and infor-mation/education. This involves linking library user needs with the appro-priate educational or service provider such as a school, health center, or career assessment institute. As we look to the future, it is safe to say that libraries will assume an even greater role in the lives of adults.

An Innovative Example

One innovative example of emerging adult education library service is the W. K. Kellogg Foundation's project known as Intermountain Community Learning and Information Services (Whitson, 1989, p. 110). The W. K. Kellogg Foundation has been a strong supporter of libraries and adult and continuing education for more than forty years. In 1985, after several years of planning and proposals, the foundation funded a four-year project to respond to the information and education needs of rural communities through programs and services delivered by new technologies and traditional methods. Local public libraries are the focus of the project with cooperative links to land-grant universities, state libraries, Cooperative Extensions, and other state, regional, and national resources. The project involves the four intermountain states of Colorado, Montana, Utah, and Wyoming. While all rural Americans share common inconveniences and disadvantages not readily apparent to their urban neighbors, mountain ranges, vast distances, hazardous winter travel, and small populations intensify the isolation felt in these four states. Ideally, rural residents should have the same access to education and information as city-dwellers, but in reality that just is not so. This project was developed to determine whether those conditions could be improved.

Wyoming project personnel developed a model to define the project more graphically. The idea of a web seemed the best way to describe the complexities and interdependence of all levels of the project (see Figure 1). The organization is not vertical or horizontal but suggests an image of concentric circles operating from the inside out and the outside in. The rural adult is the focus of the model, and the circles represent layers of people and resources to facilitate meeting the information and education needs of the rural population. Blank spaces and circles were left to indicate possibilities for expansion and additions such as new partners and even new states. It is essentially a brokering model. In each state two pilot sites are located in a rural public library. The library employs a community information specialist who serves as a channel through which needs are identified and information and education flow. According to Dr. Arlon Elser, educational program officer for the W. K. Kellogg Foundation, "The bottom line of this project is whether or not we make a difference in the lives of these rural people" (Arlon Elser, pers. comm., 1988).

The project has completed its initial funding period and has been evaluated as a whole and state by state. A long list of the project's accomplishments include credit and noncredit course delivery in the four states through the local public libraries, establishment of new literacy programs including a literacy in the local jail project, cooperative purchases of technologies to deliver information and education, public access to computers, local data-base search capabilities, and on and on. But more important to the success of the program is acceptance of this concept as valid and worthwhile. In Wyoming the project is being continued in the local libraries as service to the broader community beyond Kellogg support. Similar activities are underway in other states as well.

Conclusion

New ideas for cooperative efforts between libraries and adult education must continue to be explored. We must take the risk of going against

Figure 1. Intermountain Community Learning and Information Services: The Wyoming Program

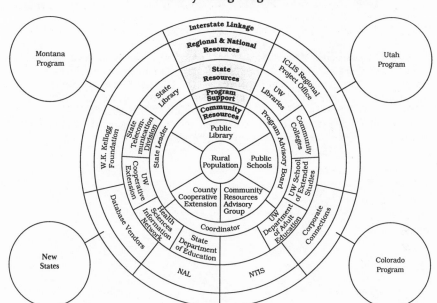

tradition to propose radical rethinking of our operations. We need a vision of the future, and now is the time to question our assumptions about past and present ways of working together and use our imaginations to prepare for the future. In some locations, especially in rural areas, the library may be the only educational opportunity available in the community. As information becomes increasingly more valuable and even essential to success in the modern world, libraries will become an even more dynamic force in the education of adults in a community. Libraries have always been social agencies playing many roles in the community. If the library is to remain the people's university, its role as disseminator of education and information will continue to increase.

References

Johnson, A. *The Public Library—A People's University*. New York: American Association for Adult Education, 1938.

Knowles, M. *A History of the Adult Education Movement in the United States*. Malabar, Fla.: Krieger, 1977.

Learned, W. S. *The American Public Library and the Diffusion of Knowledge*. San Diego, Calif.: Harcourt Brace Jovanovich, 1924.

Lee, R. E. *Continuing Education for Adults Through the American Public Library 1833–1964*. Chicago: American Library Association, 1966.

McDaniel, R. H. (ed.). *Barriers to Rural Adult Education: A Survey of Seven Northwest States*. Pullman: Washington State University Press, 1986.

Maurois, A. "Public Libraries and Their Mission." In *UNESCO Bulletin for Libraries*, no. 4. Paris: UNESCO, 1961.

Rose, E. *The Public Library in American Life*. New York: Columbia University Press, 1954.

Shera, J. H. *Foundations of the Public Library: The Origins of the Public Library Movement in New England 1629–1855*. Chicago: University of Chicago Press, 1949.

Smith, J. C. "Public Librarian Perceptions of Library Users as Self-Directed Learners." Unpublished doctoral dissertation, Syracuse University, 1990.

Whitson, D. L. "Academic Libraries and the Future of Education and Information for Rural Adults: A Model." In J. Fennell (ed.), *Building on the First Century*. Cincinnati, Ohio: Association of College and Research Libraries, 1989.

Burton R. Sisco is assistant professor of adult education at the University of Wyoming.

Donna L. Whitson is University of Wyoming Libraries assistant director for outreach services and an adjunct professor in adult education.

The church, as educator, serves as an agent of transformation for the individual, the group, and society at large.

The Educative Role of Religious Institutions

Paulette T. Beatty, Barbara P. Robbins

Religious communities fulfill a unique role in the education of their membership. The church is educator. No other description more aptly identifies the task of faith groups as they come together in community. Whatever the mode of delivery, the fundamental mission of religious institutions is inextricably linked with the educative process as it occurs in the lives of individual members.

Researchers have spoken of this fundamental mission in numerous ways (Chalfant, Beckley, and Palmer, 1987; O'Dea and Aviada, 1983). Beatty and Robbins (in press) have described the practical embodiment of the educative role of the church in current practice. They suggest that the church serves best when it stands by individuals as they move through life events, helps them in the search for meaning and order in life, guides them as they shape belief systems in light of a spiritual tradition, aids them in the critical examination of societal values, supports them as they affirm themselves as part of a religious tradition, and fosters their human growth and maturation.

This chapter addresses the educational agenda of the church in both sacred and secular arenas. We will describe the approaches employed in developing programs for adults and facilitating the learning process and will identify the constituencies involved in the diverse array of programs offered by the church. For each of these topics, a question will be posed and several strategies will be suggested for those involved in adult education in religious institutions as they review their programs. Further, we suggest a framework for exploring the potential contribution of adult education programs in the church. In conclusion, we consider the role of the church as it creates communities of lifelong learners.

NEW DIRECTIONS FOR ADULT AND CONTINUING EDUCATION, no. 47, Fall 1990 © Jossey-Bass Inc., Publishers

The Agenda

A primary component of adult education in church bodies focuses upon the explicit religious content deemed central within a given tradition. Further, programs frequently address the exercise of responsible membership within the religious community and emphasize the application of explicitly religious content in the community at large. Within this threefold focus, the sacred and the secular are interwoven as the church relates to individual members, to the faith community, and to society at large. The church offers a message that fosters personal growth and development, encourages fellowship within the religious tradition, and directs individual and corporate service within a societal context.

A brief review of denominational publications highlights the basic intent of adult religious education today (Beatty and Hayes, 1989). The Lutheran church, Missouri Synod (Constein, 1980), addresses the issue of adult education within the framework of five specific goals for learning: reading, interpreting, and integrating scripture; understanding denominational doctrines; improving interpersonal relations; applying personal convictions to daily living; and confronting societal issues. The Union of American Hebrew Congregations (1988) cites ten educational goals for their Jewish Reform tradition: Jewish identity, the law and the commandments, the state of Israel, the Hebrew language, prayer, social justice, the Jewish holidays and festival observances, respect for self and others, kinship with Jews worldwide, and synagogue support and participation. Three priorities cited by the United States Catholic Conference (1986) are assisting individuals and religious communities in living the gospel message, preparing believers to explore contemporary issues in light of the gospel, and enabling adults to become exemplars of the faith for successive generations.

There is a global question relating to the agenda for adult education programs in church settings: To what degree are the multiple functions of adult education addressed in the local congregation? From this question, a number of specific programs ensue. Comprehensive educational programs offer a spiraled or multilayered curriculum tailored to the developmental needs of members throughout the life span. The educational curriculum of the church, ideally, addresses the religious dimension, advances the spiritual growth and development of individuals, and binds families and intergenerational units. Well-designed programs move beyond information access to the level of genuine engagement as members become involved in specific outreach ministries defined by the congregation. Creative programs additionally provide a forum for the critical review of social mores and social policy.

The Procedures

Diversity characterizes both the instructional and the programming procedures employed in the delivery of adult education offerings in church settings.

Instructional procedures include how people are grouped, where programs are offered, and what instructional practices are used. Professional religious educators describe a broad range of processes being employed in a flexible manner in the delivery of adult education programs in the church. Most approaches involve small or large group instruction with little reference to self-directed learning, to one-on-one mentoring, or to individualized plans for personal growth and faith development. Within the small group setting, one typically encounters lectures, discussions, and collective reading activities augmented, on occasion, by audiovisual presentations. In the midst of these typical delivery procedures, there also exists a great diversity of program formats: instruction within worship services, Sunday schools, retreats, revivals, study circles, and prayer breakfasts, to name but a few. Instruction most frequently occurs in institutional facilities, but it may also take place in schools, homes, retreat centers, camps, and other community-based facilities (Beatty and Hayes, 1989; Beatty and Robbins, in press).

Programming procedures, though frequently not systematically addressed or fully planned, reveal a consistent pattern of practices. Responses from denominational leaders suggest some of the principles appropriate to the educative role of the church today. They reveal that exemplary programs at the local level are grounded in the present and emergent needs of individuals, institutions, and communities. They are clear about the program's basic purposes and applicability to events of everyday life. They are structured appropriately for group size, available facilities, and instructional resources. They are fiscally stable and responsible. They are targeted to attract diverse learning groups, are adequately staffed by committed and trained personnel, and are periodically evaluated (Beatty and Hayes, 1989; Beatty and Robbins, in press).

There is a global question relating to the procedures employed in the education of adults at the congregational level: Are instructional and programming procedures applied appropriately to ensure quality learning experiences for all adults? From this question, a number of specific program directions ensue.

Excellence in the teaching/learning transaction is fostered when instructional strategies are flexible, and critically selected, in order to accommodate different program objectives and unique learner groups. Further, in determining which instructional strategies to employ, it is necessary to give consideration to the realistic constraints and possibilities of the physical environment, the learning climate, and the instructional resources and personnel.

In terms of programming, excellence is fostered when a number of the following initiatives have been undertaken. A participatory structure is integrated into planning procedures for adult groups. Significant attention is given to the creation of learning climates conducive to exploration, inquiry, and personal commitment. Needs and interests of specific populations are ascertained in advance of the program. Goals, content, and methodologies, the heart of the educational program, are effectively integrated. Targeted promotional activities encourage participation. Leaders, support staff, and volunteers are adequately prepared for each program. Visionary leaders at the local level apprise themselves of the real cost of religious education programming and work to ensure a strong financial base from which to operate a viable, ongoing program. A formalized evaluation system is developed to enable value judgments regarding program directions.

The Constituencies

Most adult religious education leadership at the local level is provided by priests, ministers, rabbis, or other professionally employed religious educators. For lay leadership development, denominations have initiated either formal certification programs or less structured offerings to meet the needs of new part-time and intermittent lay volunteers. The continuing professional development needs of both professional and lay educational leaders are typically met by an array of short courses, seminars, directed reading programs, and retreats. One of the emerging challenges faced by the church today is that of training highly committed lay leadership.

Participants in adult education activities of the church tend to be members of the local congregation or part of its extended "family." Although it is difficult to ascertain the percentage of members who actually participate in adult education offerings outside of worship, a broad spectrum of the membership is represented in the general adult education program as well as in the more specialized or focused undertakings. Increasingly, programs are being developed for particular segments of the congregation or the community, including such populations as senior adults, intergenerational family groups, semi-literate adult groups, singles, women with preschoolers, young adults, divorced or separated individuals, the recently widowed, people in recovery from addictive behavior, new job entrants, parents, social action groups, and other special groups.

There is a global question relating to the constituencies involved in the adult education programs offered through local initiatives: To what degree are all members of the congregation involved in the adult education program, whether as participants or leaders? This question challenges church educators to consider whether program participants are engaged in a process of growth and development by reason of their participation in educational programs. Further, adult participants need opportunities through which they can learn to become leaders and exercise that leadership within the faith community. As participants assume increasingly active roles in directing their own ongoing agendas for learning and personal growth, the individual, the church, and the community at large all benefit. This is especially true when leadership is viewed from the perspective of service rather than power.

Toward a Learning Community

The potential of adult religious education, with its multifaceted agenda, its facilitative procedures, and its diverse constituencies, is realized only within a complex interweaving of both sacred and secular realities as perceived by individual members, the faith community, and society at large. Programs necessarily focus upon addressing the learning agendas of individuals in the community of faith. However, this agenda also focuses on shaping the faith community and transforming society itself.

When the church's educational program stands by people in life events, whether positive or negative, they are enabled to function in constructive and healthy ways. Additionally, they can be helped to think in new ways and place these life events in a larger perspective. This seldom occurs in isolation; rather, it generally takes place in small learning and support groups. Therefore, individual learning, enhanced by the group experience, can ultimately be directed toward service beyond the religious community. For example, people experiencing bereavement frequently are helped initially on a personal basis. Subsequently, through sharing this experience in an educational program targeted to address issues in the bereavement process, a support community is formed. Ultimately, this support community continues the healing process for its individual members and additionally has the potential of becoming an agent for healing others. To the degree that a commitment is made to move beyond the support structure and the faith community, the educational enterprise serves the needs of the broader community.

When the church's educational program helps people discover meaning and order in life, the church provides an interpretive structure to assist them in defining themselves in the world and in fashioning their responses to that world. Educatively, this process begins early in life and continues throughout the life span. In adult education programs, the church can help people to explore their vocations in life and to discern the challenges they offer. Consequently, people are assisted in the exercise of responsibilities commensurate with appropriate social roles. Discovering meaning in one's vocation is rarely achieved in isolation. Rather, meaning is often explored and expanded in group learning experiences and ultimately expressed productively through avenues of service in the community. For example, when a person is struggling to overcome addictive behavior that disrupts effective functioning, he or she may seek the help of a church-sponsored twelve-step educational program to establish control in his or her life. The culmination of such participation involves a spiritual awakening and a willingness not only to practice what has been learned but to carry the message to others. Thus what starts out as individual healing directs participants beyond individual and small-group learning activities to addressing the concerns of the community at large.

When the church's educational program helps shape individual belief systems in light of spiritual tradition, people develop a firm foundation for judging their moral and ethical stance in the world. This anchoring is fostered through participation in the life of worship and instruction, through individual prayer, and most visibly from an educational perspective through participation in adult learning experiences. For example, when intergenerational family units participate in learning activities that foster understanding of faith connections inherent in traditional religious seasons and celebrations, individual learning occurs. Additionally, family units are strengthened and the community of faith reaffirms its identity and finds avenues for expression of that identity in the secular arena.

When the church's educational program provides guidance for the critical examination of societal values, people are assisted in taking a stance with regard to social norms, mores, and policy. They are challenged to recognize societal needs and problems and are guided toward skillful participation in shaping the social order. In an adult education program exploring poverty and its many manifestations in our society, individual consciousness is raised. It is further tested in the context of others' opinions and ultimately evaluated in terms of the scriptural and doctrinal mandates of the religious tradition. In this context, education is not neutral but flows naturally into a proactive involvement directed toward addressing social inequities.

When the church's educational program helps people affirm themselves as part of a religious tradition, a concept of self-worth and a concept of self in relation to others emerge. Each religious tradition fosters a sense of belonging and a sense of the importance of each individual. This community and the diverse talents of its members are then placed at the service of others. For example, an urban telephone crisis ministry emerged from a commitment of several counselors and social workers to train interested lay volunteers within a local congregation. Through this process, volunteers were personally able to affirm new and emergent talents, were able to place in perspective many developmental issues within their own lives, and were actively engaged in addressing issues related to responsible adult choices.

When the church's educational program helps people accomplish the developmental tasks of human growth and maturation, it assists them in realizing their fullest potential. People typically begin this process and continue it throughout their lives. As young adults enter the work force and begin to assume responsible roles in their respective settings, challenges emerge to test their fundamental values. Life-style decisions are being made. Support in reviewing decisions during this crucial stage can be provided through small-group educational programs. This review can forge a strong consensus among the members and provide solidarity as one faces the new world. This collective energy can thus be harnessed for subsequent initiatives leading to transformation in the world of work.

Envisioning the Future

The church, as educator, serves as an agent of transformation for the individual, the group, and society at large. The educational program cannot afford to become insular and parochial. Rather, it must speak to the issues, concerns, and aspirations of the surrounding community and its institutions. Likewise, individual leaders in the adult educational programs of local congregations cannot afford to focus exclusively upon their own congregational agenda. They cannot afford to use only those instructional and programming strategies traditionally employed in their own programs. And they cannot afford to limit involvement in educational programs to members of their own congregation or fail to use local leadership resources. The establishment of communitywide, intradenominational, and interdenominational associations of adult religious educators fosters creative dialogue and a sharing of expertise that indirectly yet inevitably enhance all of the educational programs involved. The establishment of linkages with an array of provider systems, educational and noneducational, at the local level and beyond connects those systems that are positioned to respond to local needs.

The church, as an institution, is by its very nature committed to community and cannot conceivably function outside that context. Consequently, when the church and its educational program are linked in some manner to society at large, it expands its capacity for responsive and relevant programming.

References

Beatty, P. T., and Hayes, M. T. "Religious Institutions." In S. B. Merriam and P. M. Cunningham (eds.), *Handbook of Adult and Continuing Education.* San Francisco: Jossey-Bass, 1989.

Beatty, P. T., and Robbins, B. P. "Churches and Religious Education." In M. W. Galbraith and P. A. Sundet (eds.), *Education in the Rural American Community: A Lifelong Process.* Malabar, Fla.: Krieger, in press.

Chalfant, H. T., Beckley, R. E., and Palmer, C. E. *Religion in Contemporary America.* Palo Alto, Calif.: Mayfield, 1987.

Constein, B. *Adults Who Learn and Like It: A Guide for Workers in the Sunday School.* St. Louis, Mo.: Concordias, 1980.

O'Dea, T., and Aviada, J. O. *Sociology of Religion.* (2nd ed.) Englewood Cliffs, N.J.: Prentice Hall, 1983.

Union of American Hebrew Congregations. *To See the World Through Jewish Eyes: Guidelines for Adult Jewish Studies.* New York: Union of American Hebrew Congregations, 1988.

United States Catholic Conference. *Serving Life and Faith: Adult Religious Education and the American Catholic Community.* Washington, D.C.: United States Catholic Conference, 1986.

Paulette T. Beatty is program leader and associate professor of adult and extension education at Texas A&M University.

Barbara P. Robbins is a research associate at the Texas Center for Adult Literacy and Learning and a doctoral candidate in adult and extension education at Texas A&M University.

*Community-based educational programs attract a diversity of older
learners because of the flexible nature of community organizations.*

Community Education
for Older Adults

Brad Courtenay

Community-based organizations have a long and distinguished record of
providing educational opportunities for older adults. Nearly thirty years
ago, Donahue (1956) reported the results of a national study of organizations that provide education for older people. The range of providers
extends from universities to welfare departments, including such community-based organizations as community centers, recreation departments,
churches, libraries, and voluntary social agencies. These same organizations
are among the most prominent locations for educational activities for the
elderly today primarily because of their ability to respond in alternative
ways to the diverse learning needs of older students.

Characteristics of the Older Learner

To understand the appeal of community-based organizations to older adults
is to understand the nature of older learners. The use of the term *older
learners* is an appropriate point of departure, because these words imply
that older persons engage in learning activities. The gerontological research
literature abounds with studies that confirm the capability for learning by
older people without severe brain damage (Birren and Schaie, 1990). Thus,
community-based organization staff can confidently assume that their older
participants have maintained their learning ability.

The plural term *learners* is used here because there is such diversity
within the older population. On the one hand, there are older learners
with graduate degrees, stable to comfortable incomes, and excellent health.
On the other hand, some older students have little or no formal education,

NEW DIRECTIONS FOR ADULT AND CONTINUING EDUCATION, no. 47, Fall 1990 © Jossey-Bass Inc., Publishers

only a subsistence-level income, and poor health. In between are older learners with innumerable combinations of characteristics, including such factors as family configuration (married, widowed, divorced, separated, no children, some children, many children), social support systems outside the family, living arrangements, and racial and ethnic composition. Consequently, the average older learner does not exist; in reality, there are numerous subgroups of older people with definitive preferences for what and where they wish to learn.

While several studies conclude that older adults participate in educational experiences because they are sincerely interested in learning (Courtenay, 1989), no single subject attracts a majority of older learners. Participation studies of the elderly indicate significant enrollments in liberal arts courses in colleges and universities, but there is also substantial matriculation in courses that provide a sense of control or the ability to cope: physical education, health care, sciences, business, home economics, and vocational education. Obviously, such diversity of interests cannot be fulfilled in a single organization such as a university or college. The diverse nature of older adults helps to explain the wide range of educational providers that is necessary to meet their needs.

Nature of Community Education Organizations

Ventura (1982) notes three major categories of institutions that provide educational experiences for older adults. The first—educational institutions—includes colleges and universities, community and technical colleges, and nonprofit independent educational organizations. The second category is labeled community-based organizations—defined as a community or senior center, an area agency on aging, a public library, a church, or a museum. The final category of organizations is simply called "other sponsors," such as national voluntary organizations, state departments of education, and unions.

The most frequently used institution is the community-based organization. According to Ventura's analysis of the 1981 National Center for Education Statistics (NCES), most older adults (24.1 percent) take courses at community-based programs. Colleges and universities are the second major locus for older learner participation (20.8 percent). Several favorable characteristics account for the popularity of the community-based organizations with older students: location, schedule of programs, nature of program offerings, and format of offerings.

Location. Perhaps more than any other factor, the location of a program is vitally important to older adults. Older people prefer a site that is in the immediate community and near their residence. Participation is enhanced if the organization is also familiar to the older student.

Community-based organizations are generally dispersed throughout the community because their primary mission is to be responsive to all of the residents. Consequently, they are located in close proximity to members of the community, including older members. Thus, community-based organizations become specifically identified as resources for the public, providing residents a sense of ownership of places such as senior centers. In effect, natural links are formed between the community dwellers and the organization simply by virtue of the fact the program is perceived as existing for the community at large.

A related aspect of location is awareness of the organization. Fisher (1986) discovered that one of the best predictors of participation in educational programs by older adults is awareness of the location. Community-based organizations would appear to have an advantage in this respect due to their proximity and exposure within the community.

Schedule of Programs. One of the most well-documented variables regarding the participation of older students is the time of day for scheduling an educational opportunity. Almost without exception older adults prefer programs that are offered from late morning to mid-afternoon during the week. Such a schedule provides enough time in the early morning to ease into the day and sufficient sunlight for returning home in the afternoon. Although early morning sessions are not ignored, evening sessions are nearly always underattended because older adults dislike being out after dark, find it more difficult to drive at night, or live alone and fear the return to an empty house.

Since community-based organizations are mandated to be responsive to the needs of the community, they must maintain a flexible schedule. The availability of alternative scheduling makes the community-based organization especially accommodative of the needs of the older learner. Beginning times between 9:30 and 10:30 A.M. at senior centers are no mere coincidence.

Nature of Program Offerings. Among the barriers to participation in educational experiences by older adults are the policies of the institution (Cross, 1981). For example, some colleges and universities that allow older adults to enroll in credit-toward-a-degree courses tuition-free on a space available basis also require admission test scores, matriculation into a specific academic program when enrollment is at a peak, and inconvenient parking. Community-based organizations have the advantage of overcoming such barriers because they are not under educational accreditation/standards requirements, do not need extensive registration procedures, and have nearby parking or free transportation in the case of a senior center. Most important, community-based organizations are used to working with older learners.

The type of educational offering is another aspect of the program at a community-based organization. As noted above, older adults have a diversity of interests and needs; thus, the extent to which an organization is flexible in its educational opportunities is likely to enhance participation.

While community-based organizations do not have the resources to offer every type of educational experience, they do have the flexibility to provide a wide range of subject matter. For example, the "Adventures in Learning" program in the Life Enrichment Service in Atlanta, Georgia, a local affiliate of the national association of such groups, offers a weekly series of courses ranging from woodworking to a study of Shakespeare's plays. The program indicates a response to a variety of needs as categorized by McCluskey (n.d.): survival (basic car maintenance and emergency procedures); coping (guided discussion about loneliness); expressive (preparing to be a clown); contributive (working with immobile older adults); influential (advocacy in politics); and transcendent (learning to speak a foreign language).

Format of Programs. While there is little research regarding the preferred teaching techniques for older students, the anecdotal literature indicates that a variety of instructional methods are effective with older learners—depending on the subject matter, the educational level, and the learning objectives (Courtenay, 1989). Many older adults opt for an informal setting led by an expert who is sensitive to the learner's need to have some interaction with the subject through discussion and practice. These older learners are more satisfied with a balanced format rather than a session requiring complete passivity or one that requires total engagement without guidance. On the other hand, a number of older students learn best in a more dependent mode, preferring the expert who accepts primary responsibility for the learning experience (Courtenay, 1989). While this approach might be considered inappropriate for adult learning, some older participants dislike any other format.

The community-based organization offers the older student a variety of learning formats ranging from a casual environment to a formal classroom setting. This assertion is illustrated within a single organization like the "Adventures in Learning" program mentioned earlier. Each quarter, the organization offers a lecture series on current topics especially relevant to older adults. The session is led by a local expert who speaks for most of the hour, although ample time is provided for those who wish to ask questions. Simultaneously, other older learners are engaged in discussing issues important to women or busily learning how to apply paint to a canvas. In a senior center, some participants may be enrolled in a basic literacy class while others enjoy the nostalgic effects of a life review writing class. The significant point is that a community-based organization can be responsive to different learning formats and thus enhance its appeal to the older student.

Sample Profiles of Community-Based Organizations

Just as there is no single profile of the older learner, there is no single type of community-based organization. While the following profiles of community-based organizations are not intended to be exhaustive, the descriptions do provide a representative overview of the diversity of these organizations.

Community Centers. These locations serve multiple audiences in the community, including older adults. The Jewish Community Center in Rockville, Maryland, boasts a successful educational program for older adults called the Senior Seminar Program. The major objectives of the program are "to offer high-level subject matter to older adults taught by retired professionals in a noncompetitive atmosphere and to afford retired older adults the opportunity to be productive as teachers and enrich the lives of other older adults" (Ventura, 1982, p. 40). Classes range from creative writing to discussion of foreign relations. Instructors are professionals who share their expertise on a volunteer basis.

Senior Centers. With occasional exceptions, these locations are exclusively for older residents in the community. Many have financial support to provide transportation for those who cannot drive or have no other form of transport; usually, these centers rely on substantial public funds to support program activities. The Waxter Center for Senior Citizens in Baltimore, Maryland, supported primarily through public grants, is a multipurpose center that offers educational programs among its services to older citizens (Ventura, 1982). The goals of the educational program are to increase life enrichment (enjoyment and growth) and to improve the life skills (ability to cope with problems) of older learners. The classes appeal to a wide range of interests from the humanities to law and insurance. The instructional staff includes Waxter employees and volunteers, community college faculty, public school teachers, and personnel from the recreation department. Many older adults are among the instructional staff.

Shepherd Centers are senior centers funded predominantly by local churches and nominal dues paid by the membership. These centers, like their public counterparts, offer educational and service activities. The centers emerged from a model begun in Kansas City in 1972 (Sancier and Heath, 1990). The Adventures in Learning program, the educational component of the project, provides courses on a wide variety of subjects as noted earlier. Instructors are a mix of volunteers from the community, including older adults.

Area Agency on Aging. This community-based organization is located in several areas in each state. Its primary purpose is to develop and coordinate federal and state-supported service programs for older adults. Such services as senior centers, home health care, recreation programs, and nutrition sites are administered by area agencies on aging. In some instances, education components are added to the nutrition programs. Located in Phoenix, Arizona, the Peer Nutrition Education for the Elderly program, administered by the Area Agency on Aging, Region 1, is an example. The objectives of the program are to provide sessions that focus on foods necessary for daily nutritional needs and to offer meaningful ways for older adults to transfer learning into "nutritionally sound dietary patterns" (Ventura, 1982, p. 47). Class topics include nutrition, foods, consumer education, and other health issues. The lessons are offered in English, Spanish, and Chinese. Senior aides employed by the agency comprise the instructional staff.

Public Library. SAGE/Service to the Aging is an educational program administered by the Brooklyn Public Library, New York (Ventura, 1982). The purpose of this program is to increase the reading frequency level and use of the public library of older adults. In addition to emphasis on reading through book talks, film programs, and book lecture/discussions, the library provides space for classes conducted by the New York City Technical College and sponsors recreational and cultural events. Besides the faculty from local colleges and agencies, some older adults are on the instructional staff.

Churches. In almost every community there are churches that offer educational opportunities for older adults. The trend is not denomination-specific, judging from the offerings listed in Protestant, Catholic, and Jewish local newsletters. One illustrative program is the Central Club sponsored by the Central Presbyterian Church in Athens, Georgia. The objective of the program is to offer learning experiences that will enhance the knowledge and skill of older people for improving their adaptation to aging and their quality of life. The program includes informal classes on topics ranging from aerobics to mastering word-processing skills. Participants also enjoy field trips to cultural events and historical sites. An older adult volunteer administers the program; instructors often include older people.

Enhancing Lifelong Learning in the Community

Community-based educational programs offer many advantages to older adults and, by emphasizing a few activities, community providers could enhance the promotion of lifelong learning in communities. For example, increasing the opportunities for intergenerational exchanges in the educational programs would expose different generations to new perspectives about one another. Younger adults, adolescents, and children have different attitudes about older people once they have experienced an educational event together. Not only do younger generations realize that older adults are interested in learning and can in fact learn, but they also become aware that experience plays an important role in the way the learner interprets the subject under study.

Of equal importance, older adults discover that the young have serious concerns and can provide new ways to learn, for example, computer-assisted instruction. As a result, both generations have the opportunity to appreciate the importance of learning at all ages and for all types of people.

A second emphasis for community-based organizations in the future is to concentrate time and energy on marketing strategies that promote the advantages of involvement in educational programs. Testimonies by satisfied participants in the print and visual media may motivate the interested but wavering potential participant. Such publicity also extends to the entire community the value of education for older adults.

Finally, community-based organizations could enhance lifelong learning in the community by increasing emphasis on training for staff. A recent study of geriatric instruction in the United States cited the inadequate preparation of faculty and service providers in gerontology to meet future needs (Peterson, Bergstone, and Douglass, 1988). Training for service providers is haphazard at best and offered by a variety of vendors with varying levels of quality. Helping staff to understand the value of education to older persons—and to understand the staff members' own aging—expands the support for lifelong learning in the community.

Conclusion

Older adult learners are so diverse that no single organization has the ability to respond to their varied educational needs. However, community-based organizations have been successful in attracting older people because the programs are held in accessible and familiar locations, scheduled at convenient times, offer a variety of learning events, and use multiple learning formats. Flexibility is the characteristic common to all types of community-based programs, including those offered by community or senior centers, area agencies on aging, public libraries, and churches. Because of their success in serving older adults, community-based organizations have the potential to demonstrate that learning is critical to all age groups. By increasing intergenerational programs, expanding marketing efforts in the community, and promoting consistent training for staff, community-based educational programs will improve the chances for institutionalizing lifelong learning in the community.

References

American Association of Retired Persons. "A Profile of Older Americans: 1989." Washington, D.C.: American Association of Retired Persons/Administration on Aging, 1989.

Birren, J. E., and Schaie, K. W. (eds.). *Handbook of the Psychology of Aging.* (3rd ed.) San Diego, Calif.: Academic Press, 1990.

Courtenay, B. C. "Education for Older Adults." In S. Merriam and P. Cunningham (eds.), *Handbook of Adult and Continuing Education.* San Francisco: Jossey-Bass, 1989.

Cross, K. P. *Adults as Learners.* San Francisco: Jossey-Bass, 1981.

Donahue, W. "Learning, Motivation, and Education of the Aging." In J. E. Anderson (ed.), *Psychological Aspects of Aging.* Washington, D.C.: American Psychological Association, 1956.

Fisher, J. C. "Participation in Educational Activities by Active Older Adults." *Adult Education Quarterly,* 1986, *36* (4), 202–210.

McCluskey, H. Y. "Education for Aging: The Scope of the Field and Perspectives for the Future." In S. Grabowski and W. D. Mason (eds.), *Learning for Aging*. Washington, D.C.: Adult Education Association/USA, n.d.

Peterson, D. D., Bergstone, D., and Douglass, E. *Employment in the Field of Aging: The Supply and Demand in Four Professions*. Washington, D.C.: Association for Gerontology in Higher Education, 1988.

Sancier, B., and Heath, A. "Learning Opportunities for Older Adults: By Drift or by Design." Paper presented at the 16th annual meeting of the Association for Gerontology in Higher Education, Kansas City, Mo., March 1–4, 1990.

Ventura, C. "Education for Older Adults: A Catalogue of Program Profiles." Washington, D.C.: National Council on the Aging, 1982.

Brad Courtenay is associate professor and head of the Adult Education Department at the University of Georgia.

Human service organizations provide educational opportunities to clients, but these agencies often find themselves providing learning opportunities for staff as well.

Human Service Organizations as Communities of Learning

Victoria J. Marsick

Human service organizations have always been with us. In their earliest form, they were often run by religions or governments as "homes" of last resort or as a means to protect the public from real or perceived affronts. Although still frequently managed by the public sector or by not-for-profit agencies, human services today are typically staffed by professionals and oriented toward development rather than detention. They include, for example, public health and mental health facilities, the criminal justice system, welfare and rehabilitation agencies, and providers of social services. Hospitals provide human services even though they are not always run on a nonprofit basis. One could even make a case for including schools and churches in this definition since they both provide social services to the community.

It is difficult to generalize about the role of human service organizations in building communities of learners because of the diversity of this sector. Each organization is driven by the policies and beliefs of those who established it, by funding sources, and, most especially, by the people who serve on its board and staff. Despite their diversity, however,

I have been assisted in writing this chapter by several graduate students who have worked in the sectors described and are studying these agencies for their doctoral dissertations: Merlin Lewis, who works in staff and organization development with the New York State Commission of Correction; Gayle Moller, formerly with the Broward County (Florida) public school system and currently director of the South Florida Management Development Network; Karen Stevens, an education specialist with the Hampden County Association for the Retarded; and Sally Vernon, who is a staff member of the National College of Education.

all human service organizations have been greatly affected by the professionalization of human services and, with it, an expanded role for learning—not only in working directly with clients but also in the continuous learning of staff who provide services because of the information explosion in their various professions.

First, many human service organizations have moved toward a philosophy of empowering clients rather than "helping" them. Empowerment requires a change in the thinking of both staff and clients that is frequently facilitated by training and by less formal attempts to help people understand that they must take a more active role in their own development and welfare. Thus, while an agency's primary goal may not be education, staff in these organizations often find themselves helping people to learn to achieve other goals.

To make this learning among clients possible, human service organizations may secondarily become a kind of extended family of learners—beginning with the education of a wide range of staff and volunteers so they can better provide this service. New York State's Office of Mental Health, for example, has recently begun a shift in its care philosophy from one of passive "treatment of the ill" to a consumer-oriented empowerment of clients and their families as active collaborators in wellness (Chakedis, 1990). Learning is a central part of this shift. Each of the twenty-five adult facilities and five regional offices is developing an internal training team to help staff learn a new philosophy of consumer-oriented psychiatric rehabilitation. These trainers will learn the new philosophy and methods associated with it so that they can become change agents in the system through both formal training in their own facilities and less formal communication of these changes via discussions with staff, written communication, and on-the-job interactions between trained staff and others with whom they work.

Professionals continue to keep up with new developments in their own fields and agencies. Paraprofessionals and nonprofessionals also need some of this knowledge and skill to carry out their duties. In addition, staff may bring to their jobs, or acquire in the course of their work, attitudes about their clients that are counterproductive. For example, the consumer advocacy approach of the New York Office of Mental Health described earlier requires that staff regard clients as peers with whom they share decision making. However, staff have often acquired attitudes that lead them to believe they are the experts and clients are passive recipients of staff choices. Education is being used to alter these biases. Thus, human service agencies become communities of learners internally as well as externally as they work toward meeting their goals for clients.

This chapter describes the learning that takes place in the human service sector, both for staff and for clients. Several typical human service organizations are used to illustrate the learning tasks in which staff engage: a mental health program, nurse-managed wellness centers, an immigrant aid community agency, a parent-school community, and a state corrections system. These examples illustrate the following characteristics of human service organizations as learning communities: empowerment of clients and staff; examination of values, norms, and assumptions; problem posing as well as problem solving; and collaborative, continuous learning that is often informal and self-directed.

Integrating the Developmentally Disabled into Communities

The field of mental health has experienced many changes over the last ten years (Chakedis, 1990). Organic causes have been discovered for some illnesses, leading to new kinds of treatment. Rehabilitation counselors have moved away from labeling clients as ill and treating them as passive partners in recovery. Court cases, legal precedents, and consumer advocacy groups have reinforced the rights of the mentally ill and the involvement of families and communities in helping them to live relatively normal lives.

An education specialist with the Hampden County (Massachusetts) Association for the Retarded describes the implications of these current trends for learning: "Historically, folks with mental retardation have often been (and sometimes still are) treated as 'eternal children'—capable of no or little growth or development, regardless of age or functioning level. This agency is convinced that this is a false assumption—rather, that all people have the capacity to learn and grow, albeit at different paces, in different contexts, and with different teaching/learning technologies" (Karen Stevens, pers. comm., 1989).

The agency does more than provide comfortable homes for the retarded. It seeks the development of these people by placing them in private homes in the community and then helps them and their caregivers to lead lives that are as close to normal as possible. The retarded attend school or work in the community, shop at grocery stores and plazas, go to the movies, or travel on the buses. The agency assists through educational intervention, casework and advocacy, respite, care-provider education, community companion services, and social events. The agency thus seeks a shift in the thinking of the communities in which the developmentally disabled live and work. People are helped to confront their stereotypes and assumptions about people with disabilities. Families, staff, and clients become active advocates for the disabled in their communities.

From the very beginning, the agency has had a strong commitment to care-provider education, not only because of state regulation but also because of the agency's philosophy that focuses on civil, legal, and other human rights. Care providers can participate in four preservice sessions, followed by classes on teaching/learning principles and practices, certification training in standard first aid, and, eventually, a wide variety of courses and workshops. The agency is also committed to staff development, within the constraints of its budget, especially to upgrade and maintain clinical skills through in-house training, clinical consultation, and participation in outside workshops.

The preservice sessions are designed to confront stereotyped thinking about caring for the retarded, as well as to provide practical skills. Some of the stereotypes examined include the ticket seller at the local movie house who is willing to let the retarded adult pay half price because he or she is "really a kid" or the "Mother Theresa" syndrome ascribed to caregivers for being "wonderful" in caring for "these people." Staff and caregivers discover that they can learn from the retarded; the relationship is reciprocal, not simply an exercise in giving. Caregiving thus provides an opportunity to examine deeply held beliefs on the part of the staff, family, and community about what it means to be normal. The "problem" as it has been defined traditionally is re-examined from many perspectives, so that eventually everyone must redefine what is problematic about the situation—that is, what it means to be normal—rather than "doing something to" a passive person who has been labeled as deficient.

Preventing Sickness and Ensuring Wellness

The move toward empowerment in health care parallels that of the mental health field (Marsick and Smedley, 1989). People are living longer, but they are beset by new waves of chronic illness and epidemics such as AIDS that require patients to take a more active role in both preventive and curative health care. Consumers have also become more critical of health care providers and thus demand more information about their illnesses and optional treatment plans. At the same time, health has become a big business in which doctors are not the only players. A variety of allied health professionals have emerged to play specialized roles that, at times, challenge the central position and judgment of the doctor.

Nurses are part of this challenge. As a profession, nursing has traditionally emphasized many of the self-care values that consumers are now demanding. Nurses also realize that they can perform many diagnostic, preventive, and educational roles formerly held by doctors. While most nurses struggle for new avenues of recognition and responsibility in traditional care settings, some nurses have chosen to practice in newly established nurse-managed centers: birthing centers, home care agencies, visiting nursing services, and community nurse-managed wellness centers. Nurse-managed centers are often based on principles of empowerment, equality, and autonomy for both staff and clients.

Fitzpatrick (1988) describes the adult education practices of four academic nurse-managed centers. Numbering from fifty to sixty-five in the United States, academic nurse-managed centers are run by universities or colleges for faculty and student research, practicums, and community service. Clientele cover the life span, although most centers concentrate on specific age groups (the elderly, pregnant mothers, children, teenagers, and so on). Staff provide education in health and nutrition (individually or in groups), health assessments and screening, health fairs, counseling, fitness programs, and support groups. Services may be provided at the wellness center, college classrooms, community facilities, residences for specific populations (such as dormitories or senior citizen centers), or people's homes. Centers typically espouse a philosophy of wellness that is at the heart of health promotion and self-care and consistent with adult education beliefs in empowerment, self-directedness, and continuous learning. As Leddy and Pepper (1985) define it, "wellness is probably best conceptualized as an active process, continuing in time, that involves initiative, ability to assume responsibility for health, value judgments, and an integration of the total individual" (pp. 156–157).

The nurse-managed centers studied by Fitzpatrick illustrate a dilemma in the creation of learning communities when staff are professionals who possess specialized knowledge and learners are, in fact, dependent on staff for a valued service they could not undertake on their own. Staff must walk a thin line between involvement of the communities in their own health education and care and the more directive role that is often taken by doctors in the medical model.

Thus, staff generally agree that the centers should be comfortable, conveniently located learning communities in which clients feel respected and welcome. Staff also understand that, for people to learn, nurses must understand and build on clients' life experiences. However, nurses find it more difficult to help learners to be self-directed and do not always think this is appropriate even though one finds examples of the use of behavioral contracts, food diaries, programmed instruction, self-evaluation, and independent study. Empowerment is a series of little victories in self-care based on information that enables people to do more for themselves, but nurses do not set out to help clients redefine their lives, social problems, or environmental concerns that might affect their health. Problems are generally identified by staff, not by clients, based on specialized knowledge. Clients might be consulted in identifying educational needs, but staff also develop programs based on their understanding of the health issues that clients in that age or care group might face: AIDS education for college students; use of the Older American Resources and Services self-assessment tool for the elderly to identify social, economic, mental health, physical health, and daily living resources; or the creation of a "reminiscing" discussion group for older clients to get them out of their apartments.

In summary, while nurse-managed wellness centers are learning communities, the mystique of the medical model can moderate the degree to which learning is initiated, directed, and sustained by clients rather than staff.

Building School-Based Learning Communities

Schools represent another kind of human service agency where professionals hold specialized knowledge yet can learn from their clients. While schools serve children, they also build learning communities for adults. Since 1968, federally funded programs have encouraged parent involvement. By 1974, the Elementary and Secondary Education Act, Title 1, had mandated parental involvement and provided funding to cover expenses parents might incur, such as transportation and child care. By 1981, the same programs required training for members of parent advisory councils. In the 1970s, states independently joined this federal fund. Principals and teachers began to invite parents to assist in strategic planning, thus moving well beyond the typical voluntarism that had been the norm. Parent advisory councils (PACs) have become commonplace in many school systems. These groups are generally composed of parents, principals, and teachers. Training for PACs typically includes organization and operation of the PAC, responsibilities of PAC members, and parenting activities.

Simultaneously, there has been a trend toward shared decision making—an effort to bring representatives from all constituencies together to design restructuring plans to improve learning. Teams of teachers, administrators, parents, and students are working together in learning communities to address the major issues facing schools. Public schools in Broward County (Florida) illustrate this trend. The eighth largest school system in the nation, the 172 school sites in this county provide educational opportunities for over 155,000 children and adults. The county has fostered community participation in decision making by setting up advisory councils and then training parents, school personnel, and community members to explore and develop the collaborative nature of this relationship.

Training is an integral component of this effort. To function well as a team, professionals learn how to include parents in their decision making and parents learn what has previously been considered professional/technical knowledge about schools and teaching. Leadership training has been provided to district-level advisory committees in order to assess leadership styles, develop skills in running effective meetings, and undertake strategic planning. These leaders have often trained community members at lower levels at the school site or in the area councils. School advisory council teams—consisting of a principal, teacher, and the council chairperson—are also helped to conduct their own planning sessions. They learn how to delineate roles and responsibilities, function effectively as a group, and develop action plans for working together. A facilitator will eventually be appointed who can provide ongoing training to members of these councils. Parents can participate in a variety of workshops and seminars—on parenting, multicultural awareness, adviser/advisee programs requiring parental participation, and Saturday schools that involve parents.

Not all schools provide as many formal training opportunities as does this example from the Florida school system. However, without structured opportunities for such learning, staff and parents may not be able to assume new roles as decision making is decentralized. The training being carried out in Florida is designed to create a community of reflective practice in which teachers are able to break down the barriers of isolation often experienced in their classrooms and to reach out to one another, principals, and parents in learning how to provide more effective education to the community. In this way, professionals and parents are being trained to continue the process of learning from one another on a daily basis as problems arise.

Reaching Out to Immigrants

The literature does not offer many examples of how community-based social service agencies can be structured as learning communities, even though writers often advocate for this position. These social service agencies are often close to their constituents, have people representative of their client group as paid or volunteer staff, and involve their clients in some way in decisions about programs. Their clients are often the people in society who are the least economically advantaged; thus, they often operate on shoestring budgets that do not permit high-technology education. Learning may be organized for clients through workshops, seminars, or courses; or it may be built into one-on-one or support group activities. As nonprofit organizations, these agencies may not have the time, resources, or expertise to organize much formal staff training. Staff often learn the ropes by watching others or rising to challenges on their jobs since there are many needs to be filled and seldom enough qualified people to fill them. Ironically industry—often admired as a leader in organizing learning for staff—is now turning to some of these same methods of learning from experience as more suitable to the fast-paced, ever-changing environment of managers (McCall, Lombardo, and Morrison, 1988).

Travelers and Immigrants Aid of Chicago is an example of a human service agency that contributes, formally and informally, to the lifelong educational opportunities of adult learners. Its mission is to provide services to people in transition. Clients are disadvantaged or disenfranchised for many reasons; they may be victims of torture or domestic violence, homeless, or immigrants. The agency provides them with legal aid, social services, education and training, and job placement. Besides survival, this population needs services that foster a sense of self and community, professional growth, and opportunity.

The agency has formed partnerships with local educational organizations to meet many of these needs in an integrated way. Community colleges, volunteer literacy organizations, and high schools, for example, address basic skill and English-language deficits. Corporations have jointly funded and conducted vocational training programs. Advocacy and social service groups provide survival skills training programs for newly arrived immigrants whose needs are immediate. Public health professionals have joined the organization as staff, volunteers, and advocates to address the health needs of the homeless and illegal aliens. The programs are offered wherever learning can take place—at the workplace, in community centers, on the street, in shelters, and in homes.

Staff in this agency employ a team approach to providing services, yet little is consciously done to teach teamwork. As in many organizations, staff learn to do this by watching others in power. At Travelers Aid, time is taken to provide these opportunities: Leaders model teamwork by sharing the dirty work as well as the glory; they give younger staff the leadership role at meetings; they hold functions at which staff meet and talk with people in various departments; and they seek out diversity in job assignments so that different perspectives are drawn upon.

Shared teaching and learning responsibility, among team members and between staff and clients, is a given. Agency clientele serve on advisory committees that establish program direction and identify learning needs. This shared decision making provides many opportunities for learning—about the problems themselves, as well as how to work more effectively together in peer relationships. Unlike many staff training programs that focus on professional development skills alone, personal development in both staff members and clients is recognized as valuable since many of the issues that clients face are reflective of personal and life decisions.

Learning to Rehabilitate the Imprisoned

The public may not think of prison systems as learning communities, yet the rehabilitation of inmates often involves literacy classes, preparation for GED exams, and vocational learning opportunities. The staff of prison systems are much like the shoemaker's children, however. When resources are scarce, money is more likely to be spent on alleviating crowded conditions and meeting prison standards than on extensive staff training, even though some training may be mandated.

Nonetheless, the Advisory Commission on Intergovernmental Relations (1984) reports that more than half the states provide some form of training for staff. In about a fifth of the states, training is delivered by state corrections agencies—agencies primarily concerned with running prisons, not jails. Because jails are funded by local governments, the tax base is generally low and jails are consequently poorly funded. As a result, state agencies are often formed to ensure that local operations meet standards; they also provide some technical assistance, including training. However, because enforcement is the agency's primary objective, the relationship between the agency and its constituents is often adversarial rather than consultative. Even though technical assistance units such as training have a friendlier relationship, training is often viewed first as a requirement and only secondarily as a benefit to the agency.

Given these circumstances, it is difficult, if not impossible, to build a learning community in the corrections field. The New York State Commission of Correction (SCOC), however, has been experimenting since 1985 with a regional training network that attempts to turn this problem around. Created in 1973, the training unit of five professionals initially tried to meet its objectives by designing customized or purchasing package programs. Courses were offered periodically on such topics as instructor development, suicide prevention, supervision and management, interpersonal communications, and inmate behavioral management. However, the staff could not meet minimum requirements, let alone their desired objectives. They could not train more than 250 officers each year in a mandated basic training course for new employees, for example, but more than three times that number required it.

Following a review in 1985, the training unit decided to develop the capacity of local staff to provide their own training, create a collaborative, consultative relationship with staff in county jails that would permit honest feedback about the quality of programs, and develop an intercounty network among jail staff to help county trainers work together to develop and deliver programs. In order to make these changes, the staff's role had to change from that of "expert" to "consultant." A new relationship had to be negotiated with county sheriffs individually and the New York State Sheriffs' Association collectively. Local staff had to learn how to deal differently with the SCOC training unit, and with each other. And the unit had to learn to work with a concept of power—collaborative, not coercive—that was out of step with the organization's culture.

The strategy used to implement this approach was to model it while at the same time working within the culture to protect this new relationship as it evolved. Training was one of the tools used, but courses were not held to "enforce" the new strategy. Instead, the core group of trainers went out and worked as consultants with the members of the network as they introduced the concept, thought it through with staff, identified needs (for training or for creating the network), codesigned activities, gave and received feedback, strategized, and dealt with obstacles to success.

Conclusion

The foregoing examples illustrate principles cited at the beginning of this chapter for building learning communities in human service agencies. A learning community seeks empowerment of clients and staff to take an active role in determining their own future. In this effort, people are helped to examine values, norms, and assumptions that underlie the way in which "service" is defined by and for them. Clients and staff engage in a process of codefining their reality, which is something like the process of problem posing discussed by Schön (1983), in which they must make sense of a complex situation before they seek solutions to it. Finally, learning may or may not be carried out through organized classes. And even when it is, a good deal of the learning takes place through collaborative, continuous learning from experience by clients or staff who pursue their own learning goals using the resources available to them.

References

Advisory Commission on Intergovernmental Relations. *Jails: Intergovernmental Dimensions of a Local Problem: A Commission Report*. Washington, D.C.: Advisory Commission on Intergovernmental Relations, 1984.

Chakedis, V. "Perceptions of Mental Health Workers of Consumer Empowerment." Dissertation proposal, Teachers College, Columbia University, 1990.

Fitzpatrick, A. A. "A Comparative Study of Principles and Practices of Adult Education in Health Education/Promotion Programs in Academic Nurse Managed Centers." Unpublished doctoral dissertation, Teachers College, Columbia University, 1988.

Leddy, S., and Pepper, J. M. *Conceptual Bases of Professional Nursing*. Philadelphia, Pa.: Lippincott, 1985.

McCall, M. W., Jr., Lombardo, M. M., and Morrison, A. M. *The Lessons of Experience: How Successful Executives Develop on the Job*. Lexington, Mass.: Heath, 1988.

Marsick, V. J., and Smedley, R. R. "Health Education." In S. Merriam and P. Cunningham (eds.), *Handbook of Adult and Continuing Education*. San Francisco: Jossey-Bass, 1989.

Schön, D. A. *The Reflective Practitioner*. New York: Basic Books, 1983.

Victoria J. Marsick is an associate professor of adult education at Teachers College, Columbia University. She has worked internationally as a staff member and consultant in staff development and training to a variety of private and public-sector agencies.

Museums provide rich and varied opportunities for lifelong learning.

Museums as Educational Institutions

Mary C. Chobot, Richard B. Chobot

There are close to five thousand museums in the United States (Chobot, 1989), ranging from world-famous institutions like the Smithsonian in Washington, D.C., to specialized local collections such as the Hall of Fame of the Trotter in Goshen, New York. In general terms, museums can be categorized as historical, scientific, or aesthetic. Some collections are general in nature, while others provide specialized coverage of a particular period or topic. Each museum provides a rich environment for lifelong learning and a variety of opportunities for adult learners.

Museums have recognized their educational mission since the early part of the twentieth century. Much of the literature on museum education has focused on programs for youth. This chapter, however, addresses the manner in which museums have sought to meet the learning needs of adults. First we will describe the unique characteristics of users that make the museum's adult education mission so challenging. Next we discuss the evolving place of education within museums. Finally, we present a sampling of the varied programs and technologies that museums currently offer to accomplish their educational mission.

Museum Users

Museum visitors range from the incidental general visitor to the person who is both interested and knowledgeable regarding some element of the institution's collection. Shepard (1989) would consider the public at large as incidental visitors with museums peripheral to their lives.

Mandle (1981) has developed an interesting matrix for museum and departmental planning. The matrix suggests three levels of public sophistication and interest in art: Level I includes the totally uninitiated, general visitor; Level II includes the visitor with some knowledge and interest; Level III includes the interested and knowledgeable visitor. For each level, he posits four levels of increasing intensity of contact with art, staff, and resources: self-directed; more sustained; high involvement; and intensely sustained. Translating this model into an adult education context, using the level of "more sustained" contact as an example, Mandle would suggest a general guided tour for the Level I visitor, a specific guided tour for the Level II visitor, and a scholarly guided tour for the Level III visitor.

Museums serve a highly diverse clientele engaged in some level of informal learning, unlike the structured, formal learning offered in traditional education institutions. Above all, such learning is voluntary, providing the added challenge of engaging and holding people's interest until they achieve the personal level of learning they seek.

Museum Education

A study by the Commission on Museums for a New Century (1984) suggests that while museums are institutions of object-centered learning, there is no accepted philosophical framework for museum education. Eisner and Dobbs (1986) reported on the results of interviews with thirty-eight museum directors in twenty large and medium-sized art museums around the United States. They found a lack of consensus on the goals and function of museum education. The role of museum educator is ill defined and perceived as lacking both substance and stature.

Schouten (1987) finds that museum educators in smaller museums often come from education or some other helping profession such as social work. Their natural programmatic orientation, in light of their prior professional experience, is toward children. By contrast, educators in larger museums are usually academically trained. As such, they are concerned primarily with objects and have little knowledge of learning strategies and needs of target audiences.

Museum Characteristics

Added to the diversity of users and the lack of consensus on the nature and role of museum education is the institutional evolution occurring in museums. Eisner and Dobbs (1986) suggest that one's perception of a museum's function and programming depends on one's conception of a museum. Table 1, introduced by Sola at a 1986 UNESCO seminar on museums and education (cited in Schouten, 1987), compares the characteristics of traditional and new museums.

Table 1. Characteristics of Traditional and New Museums

Traditional	New
Purely rational	Also takes emotions into account
Specialized	Allows complexity to become apparent
Oriented toward end product	Oriented toward processes
Emphasizes objects	Gives visible form to concepts
Oriented mainly toward the past	Also relevant to the present
Originals only	Also accepts copies
Formal approach	Informal approach
Authoritative approach	Communicative approach
Objectively scientific	Creatively popular
Conforms to existing order	Nonconformist and oriented toward renewal

Source: Cited in Schouten (1987).

This, then, is the context for adult and continuing education in museums: a varied audience, evolving institutional structures, and an emerging but not yet stabilized perspective on the role, function, and personnel requirements for museum education and museum educators. Now let us examine the variety of offerings that museums make available to the adult learner.

Museum Education and Lifelong Learning: Some Examples

In this changing educational landscape, we can expect to find rich and varied continuing education activities. Presented here is a sampling of adult continuing education programs offered by museums.

Traditional Strategies. The traditional approach to museum education includes captioned, interpretive exhibits of objects, sometimes supplemented with illustrated catalogues, guided tours, lectures, and classes such as those offered by the Associates Program of the Smithsonian Institution. Over the last decade, films and video have played an increasing role in museum education. Museums in some areas have made use of radio and public television in educational outreach.

Specialized Programming. Museums have focused on meeting the needs and utilizing the special skills of certain populations such as older Americans. For example, the New England Aquarium in Boston has a program called EldeReach, which involves an outreach session at the seniors' site followed by a field trip to the aquarium. The outreach session is used to stimulate interest in the program and create rapport between the instructor and the participants. A slide show is presented highlighting the marine life exhibited at the aquarium. Senior citizens are also encouraged to handle certain live sea creatures that are brought to the site.

The visit to the aquarium takes place on a weekday afternoon, when the facility is relatively quiet. The instructor who conducts the outreach also leads the group in what, for many, is their first visit to the aquarium. The outreach and visit also serve as a stimulus for participants to recall and share experiences they have had with the sea with each other and with the museum staff.

Elderhostel is a program that began in 1975 (Knowlton, 1977). It is a network of colleges, independent schools, environmental parks, and museums throughout the United States, Canada, and Europe that offer short residential programs for adults at least sixty years of age. Under the egis of this program, Old Sturbridge Village, a living history museum in Massachusetts, offers a program for senior citizens that involves staff members presenting one-and-a-half-hour sessions, followed by tours, on a variety of topics (such as "From Farm to Factory: A Factory's Operative's View"). The program is supplemented by hands-on activities in the museum's education building.

The Winnipeg Art Gallery established a senior citizens group called the Winnipeg Art Gallery Seniors. In 1984, membership in the program was up to six hundred. In addition to a variety of programs (art appreciation, drama workshops, art classes, music appreciation, and the like), a drop-in center provides a social outlet for members two days a week.

Older citizens are also a valuable museum cultural resource. Hunt (1984) cites an example of a 1977 initiative in connection with the Festival of American Folklife. Smithsonian folklorists brought together a group of retired railroad workers to demonstrate and talk about their work. These older adults served as an interpretive link between a railroad exhibit and the visitors.

The Lyceum, a small museum in Alexandria, Virginia, uses the personal recollections of older citizens to complement in-museum slide shows and discussions of local history. Ice cream made the "old-fashioned way" is served and artifacts are handled and discussed. This is a low-cost program that has enabled a small museum to increase both its audience and its donor base.

The Arts. Art museums have shown remarkable creativity in bringing their programs to the adult learner. Collins (1981) showcases a number of museum-based adult education initiatives. The Ringling Museums in Sarasota, Florida, organize a Medieval and Renaissance Fair to bring their excellent collection of Renaissance and Baroque objects to the attention of the public. The fair has stimulated interest in costume, language, architectural styles, crafts, games, food, art, literature, and competitions of the period.

The Royal Ontario Museum provides a coordinated museum-wide introductory program for adults. The continuing education activities include lectures, courses, field trips, and workshops. Extensive use is made of video and slides to illustrate the objects and concepts being discussed. The museum's staff believe that the presence of actual items from the collection is an important element of the continuing education program. Therefore, whenever feasible, actual artifacts and specimens are made available for viewing and, if appropriate, for handling by session participants.

The Philadelphia Museum of Art designed a seven-month program, "Art as a Reflection of Human Concerns," built around seven basic themes felt to be of interest to the public. Selected objects from the museum's collection were presented in the context of family, humor, religion, aging, death, birth, and love. A combination of activities that included speakers, gallery talks, films, and performances was used to portray each theme.

The Sciences. The Science Museum of Minnesota uses theater techniques in anthropology interpretation. Theater provides a context for the presentation of artifacts that, when detached from their setting, lack meaning for most museum visitors.

The Boston Children's Museum describes itself as a hands-on, participatory, interactive museum. It reports that approximately 45 percent of its visitors are adults. Because of the museum's orientation toward children, adults appear willing to "learn content . . . that they might otherwise find threatening" (Gurian, 1981, p. 279). Recognizing this fact, the museum has structured space and designed activities to facilitate this learning process.

History. Old Sturbridge Village is a living museum of regional New England history. In addition to the Elderhostel program described above, its Teacher Education Program is designed to foster links between the schools and the museum as an extension of the classroom. Two ten-day summer workshop sessions afford teachers the opportunity to experience the history portrayed at Old Sturbridge Village. An evaluation of the program indicates that not only does the program influence the participant's classroom activities but 75 percent of respondents continue their involvement with museums and field-based learning years after their summer workshop session.

Finally, an exemplary program of comprehensive museum adult education at Mystic Seaport, Connecticut, is described by Carr (1986). Like Old Sturbridge Village, Mystic Seaport is a living history museum complex that supports an extensive adult education program, including sailing classes on museum-owned craft, courses in marine skills such as celestial navigation, a concentrated small-boat building course, and courses in period topics such as weaving and fireplace cooking. In addition to the actual programs, videotapes and laser videodiscs allow greater access to various elements of the museum's collection. The museum also has traditional exhibits of a variety of period crafts, trades, and life-styles.

Special Focus. Some museums provide adult continuing education in highly specialized areas. The Peace Museum in Chicago focuses on issues of war and peace, human rights, social change, social justice, peacemakers, and peacemaking; it also provides an organized program for adults that includes peace education.

The Anacostia Museum in Washington, D.C., a community-based museum that is part of the Smithsonian, focuses on Afro-American history and culture. Lectures and workshops are offered throughout the year, generally related to the theme of the current exhibit—for example, the Black Church.

Several ethnic museums are located in Chicago. Among these are the Polish Museum of America, the Swedish-American Museum Association of Chicago, the Mexican Fine Arts Center Museum, and the Balzekas Museum of Lithuanian Culture. These museums offer various continuing education activities including hobby workshops, participatory exhibits, and organized educational programs for adults.

Technology and Museum Education

The use of videodiscs has been increasing in museums over the last decade. Advances in optical digital storage technologies promise to further expand educational opportunities and access to museum materials for adult learners.

Videodisc. In the past, adults wishing to take advantage of a museum's educational opportunities have had to go to the museum. The ability of the videodisc to hold up to 54,000 images or thirty minutes of motion video on a side, as well as its durability, make it a powerful medium for exporting museum materials to learners. For example, in 1984 the National Gallery of Art released for sale an award-winning videodisc that contains a gallery tour and 1,653 still images of objects in the collection. Additional examples of museum collections on videodisc are identified by Cash (1985). It should be noted, however, that videodiscs require a special player and some of the educational applications are accompanied by software and require a computer for their use.

An increasingly popular in-house museum application of videodisc technology is the interactive video kiosk, which allows users to browse, to structure their own inquiries on a given topic, and to "handle" and view rare objects. For example, at the J. Paul Getty Museum in Santa Monica, California, visitors can browse via videodisc through illuminated manuscripts prepared during the Renaissance.

Binder (1988) indicates that more than fifty museums have interactive videodisc-based displays in operation. Fritz (1990) predicts that the number of museums reporting some use of videodisc technology will double by the beginning of 1991.

Optical Digital Media. Videodisc represents a significant advance in image storage technology. However, videodisc is an analog medium. Advances in hardware and software now permit the creation of multimedia digital data bases containing higher-quality images, particularly where text is involved, and the ability to integrate and display full-motion video.

Intel Corporation is offering a technology called digital video interactive (DVI) that allows users to store, in digital form on a CD–ROM disc, combinations of text, audio, video stills, graphics, animation, and motion video. For example, one CD-ROM disc, the same size as a commercially available CD audio disc, might contain twenty minutes of full-motion video, 5,000 high-resolution stills, 15,000 pages of text, and six hours of associated audio. A computer, equipped with a special board, and a CD-ROM player are needed to display DVI. However, a stand-alone optical digital medium developed by SONY and Philips called compact disc interactive (CDI) is also commercially available.

Use of optical digital data-base technology in museums is just beginning. For example, LeBlanc (1990) describes an ongoing effort at the Ford Museum in Dearborn, Michigan, to create a digital data base containing images and descriptive data on more than 200,000 objects and 500,000 historic photographs. However, it is not outside the realm of possibility to envision this technology being used within the decade to disseminate data bases containing selected museum holdings to individuals or institutions such as libraries for use by adult learners.

Conclusion

The museum is a rich source of lifelong learning opportunities for adults. Within the last decade, the museum's potential as a learning resource has increased as a result of changing perspectives regarding the museum's role and the function and importance of museum education. Added to this are advances in image storage, retrieval, and display technology. This technology will permit the development and dissemination of learning resources that engage the museum visitor more dynamically and increase access to the collection by adult learners.

References

Binder, R. *Videodiscs and Museums*. Falls Church, Va.: Future Systems, 1988.

Carr, J. R. "Education Everywhere for Everyone at Mystic Seaport." In *The American Museum Experience: In Search of Excellence*. Edinburgh, Scotland: Scottish Museums Council, 1986.

Cash, J. "The Museum on Laser Videodisc." *Museum News*, 1985, *64*, 19–35.

Chobot, M. C. "Public Libraries and Museums." In S. B. Merriam and P. M. Cunningham (eds.), *Handbook of Adult and Continuing Education*. San Francisco: Jossey-Bass, 1989.

Collins, Z. W. (ed.). *Museums, Adults and the Humanities: A Guide to Educational Programming*. Washington, D.C.: American Association of Museums, 1981.

Commission on Museums for a New Century. *Museums for a New Century*. Washington, D.C.: American Association of Museums, 1984.

Eisner, E. W., and Dobbs, S. M. "The Mission of Museum Education." *Museum Studies Journal*, 1986, *2* (3), 10–15.

Fritz, M. "Interactive Video Becomes a Museum Piece." *CBT Directions*, 1990, *3* (5), 23–27.

Gurian, E. "Adult Learning at Children's Museum of Boston." In Z. W. Collins (ed.),

Museums, Adults and the Humanities: A Guide to Educational Programming. Washington, D.C.: American Association of Museums, 1981.

Hunt, M. "The Grand Generation: Folklore in Aging." *Roundtable Reports: The Journal of Museum Education,* 1984, *9* (4), 15-16.

Knowlton, M. P. "Liberal Arts: The Elderhostel Plan for Survival." *Educational Gerontology,* 1977, *2,* 87-94.

LeBlanc, S. A. "Delivering a Low Cost Art Museum Database." *Advanced Imaging,* 1990, *5* (6), 32-36.

Mandle, R. "Adult Programming Approaches." In Z. W. Collins (ed.), *Museums, Adults and the Humanities: A Guide to Educational Programming.* Washington, D.C.: American Association of Museums, 1981.

Schouten, F. "Museum Education—A Continuing Challenge." *Museums,* 1987, *39* (4), 240-243.

Shepard, L. B. "We Must Help the Public to Discover What Museums Have to Offer." *Museum News,* 1989, *68* (3), 79.

Mary C. Chobot is president of Mary C. Chobot and Associates, a Washington, D.C., consulting firm involved in adult and continuing education.

Richard B. Chobot is an independent consultant specializing in adult education and training.

Developing an understanding of how the mass media shape adults'
frameworks of interpretation—and how they can stimulate adults'
critical thinking—is crucial for educators.

Mass Media as Community Educators

Stephen D. Brookfield

The organization, products, and effects of the mass media—particularly
radio, television, and the press—are important phenomena to educators of
adults. In all realms of contemporary experience—from depictions of family
life to the creation of agendas for political discourse—the mass media play
a powerful role in creating the interpretive frameworks through which we
make sense of many events in our lives. Adults' structures of understanding
evolve as they interact with the various agents of socialization. While ample
attention has been paid to such agents as the family, school, religion, and
the workplace, the influence of media is only just beginning to be appre-
ciated, let alone understood. In this chapter I review the arguments over
the power the media are said to exert in contemporary communities and
then present two examples of prime-time network television programs that
seem to perform a valuable educational function in the community.

Media Power: The Debate Clarified

According to one school of thought, the mass media are used by dominant
social classes to establish their hegemony in different communities. Hegemony is the process by which public consensus about social reality is created
by those in power, so that what are perceived as "common sense" values
and beliefs in fact reflect the culture of the dominant class in the community. In totalitarian societies, citizens are subject to a continual onslaught of
symbols, messages, and information through the media—all designed to
engineer consent to the established order. This is the Orwellian nightmare
of 1984. To those who believe that the media are wholly manipulative, a

NEW DIRECTIONS FOR ADULT AND CONTINUING EDUCATION, no. 47, Fall 1990 ©Jossey-Bass Inc., Publishers primary purpose of education is to create in students an awareness of just how strongly their conventional wisdom is created and reinforced by the mass media.

The Orwellian perspective sees the mass media as villainously omnipotent shapers of thought and behavior created solely for the purpose of lulling entire populations into stupefaction. Those who subscribe to this belief regard television, radio, and the press as fronts for big business and political interests. These interests use media to divert people's minds from focusing on the inequities of capitalism. When we look at the range of television programming available in the modern American community, or at the kinds of tabloid newspapers that are by far the most widely read, it is easy to be convinced by this argument regarding the media's functions. Through an endless televisual diet of bland sit-coms and mindless game shows, and a continual focusing by newspapers on sensationalist front-page accounts of sex and violence, the mass media certainly give little indication of being a force for educational good in communities.

Yet this pessimistic determinism regarding the all-pervasive effects of the mass media can be overstated. In the face of the products of the mass media it is easy to become filled with hopeless resignation—a belief that the media are so powerful, and educators so weak, that short of preventing students from becoming contaminated through any kind of contact with the media, there is little educators can do. But to view the mass media solely as monolithic transmitters of repressive cultural values that are uncritically assimilated by passive dupes is somewhat misleading. There are three reasons why this is so: the active role people play in interpreting media messages; the elements of opposition and resistance within the media; and the ways in which educators can help adults become more critically aware of the media as a social force.

First, consumers of media are not vacuous individuals upon whom can be stamped any set of beliefs chosen by television producers or newspaper barons. When people watch television they take an active role in interpreting televisual images and narrative—agreeing with some viewpoints, rejecting others, and ignoring many completely. Generally there is a range of responses to media, including deferential decoding of media (in which people essentially agree with media depictions of reality), negotiated decoding (in which people accept some elements of media images as accurate but reject others), and oppositional decoding (in which people regard media messages as inaccurate representations supporting the positions of power occupied by dominant social groups).

Second, people within the media sometimes operate in oppositional ways. As this chapter shows, prime-time network television can sometimes produce programs that challenge prevailing stereotypes. Advertisers and executives can certainly exercise enormous power over producers, editors, writers, performers, and directors, but such power relationships are not wholly static. Stories can be produced in radio, television, and the press that present ideas and interpretations which criticize the actions of powerful interests such as governments and corporations. There is a healthy regard for the traditions of investigative journalism and the free press that continually draws on the principle of freedom of speech so beloved of Americans of all political hues.

Third, educators can help adults to become media literate—that is, help them realize that what they read, hear, and see in the mass media are cultural constructions created by individuals drawn from a certain sector of society, rather than objective depictions of reality (Brookfield, 1986). Exercises in decoding, in content analysis, and in program creation can help develop media literacy in people in a range of community settings (Berger, 1983; Logan, 1979). Indeed, if a critically informed citizenship is an essential component of democracy, then there is a national political need for a network of community media literacy groups. Such groups would help citizens decode, filter, and interpret the political messages conveyed by the mass media. Given the predominance of newspapers and television as sources of political information for most adults, there is an obvious need for educators to help adults become aware of the tendency to oversimplify and sensationalize the discussion of political issues inherent to these media.

Case Studies of Oppositional Media

In the worlds of broadcasting and the press there are many examples of media initiatives that might be described as oppositional. These initiatives are educative in that they encourage critical thinking about the products of the media. Oppositional media initiatives help to make people aware that the content of the mass media is a created reality and that there are many possible interpretations of news events in addition to those contained in mainstream reports and broadcasts. Magazines and journals such as *The Village Voice, The Nation,* and *Mother Jones* present material directly critical of the structures dominant in society or strongly disapproving of governmental actions. In television, opposition and resistance occur as producers, writers, and performers struggle to create programs that are neither purely palliative nor wholly uncritical of prevailing ideologies.

The Donahue Show. One example of how even a prime-time network television program can function in an oppositional mode—opening up alternative perspectives and interpretations that challenge the dominant culture—is the *Donahue* show. In the mid 1980s (before the advent of the Oprah Winfrey and Geraldo Rivera talk shows forced Donahue to show up wearing the occasional dress) the *Donahue* show provided a good example of how a popular talk show can undertake serious scrutiny of political issues. *Donahue* attracts a large audience, particularly of women viewers, and many of the shows deal with what producers see as popular "women's" interests: soap opera stars, cooking, aerobics, diets, and birth control. Mixed in with such popular offerings, however, have been some quietly effective attempts to promote political literacy. The list of transcripts available from the program shows that it has covered such topics as United States policy in Central America (one program featured Nicaraguan President Daniel Ortega being interviewed live by the *Donahue* audience), the negative influence of television advertising in political elections, and the importance of political satire in democracies. In the aftermath of American military interventions against Libya, Grenada, and Panama, the *Donahue* show featured guests who criticized these interventions at a time when the country seemed caught up in a fervor of nationalistic pride.

Perhaps the most striking example of an oppositional *Donahue* show (and the one that sparked the greatest volume of letters from outraged viewers) was broadcast in the summer of 1984. At this time a film titled *Seeing Red*—a documentary featuring interviews with members and ex-members of the American Communist Party—had just been released. Donahue had as his guests on the program the producer of the film and three of its prominently featured Communists. Upon introducing these individuals at the beginning of the show and detailing their past and present political allegiances, Donahue was greeted by shouts of "Send them back to Russia!" from the audience. By asking his guests to explain the moral outrage and Christian altruism that had motivated them to join the Communist Party in the aftermath of the Depression, and to discuss their disillusionment with the current state of the party, Donahue created an environment in which strongly divergent social perspectives were aired to a mass audience. During this time Donahue expressed no overt political allegiance and did not attempt to convert either his audience or his guests. He challenged his audience without making them feel personally threatened, he encouraged an examination of differing perspectives on issues, and he engaged his audience in an active exploration of experience.

Thirtysomething. A second example of educative network television deals with the domain of adult relationships. In the ABC weekly series *Thirtysomething* we have an example of a prime-time drama that breaks many prevailing televisual rules and conventions. Despite the tradition in commercial television that audiences should never be left confused or confronted by ambiguity, *Thirtysomething* refuses to provide simple solutions, happy endings, or clear prescriptions. The show depicts the messiness of adult life as realistically as could be imagined within the constraints of network television. It refuses to simplify the complex dilemmas of adult life and encourages us to empathize with the very divergent perspectives of different characters.

In terms of perspective—a central component in the development of critical thinking—*Thirtysomething* is both deft and convincing in its depiction of multiple interpretations of the same situation. Two episodes illustrate this feature admirably. In one, a social event is portrayed from the viewpoint of the chief protagonists. Nancy and Elliot, and Michael and Hope, go out for dinner and return home together. Over coffee Nancy is encouraged to perform her high school cheerleader routine. In seeing the evening unfold through the eyes of both Nancy and Elliot we realize just how unequivocally our perceptual filters interpret—and grant very different meanings to—the same events. In Elliot's eyes the evening begins with a coquettish Nancy teasing him sexually, arousing him against his will, and then insensitively rejecting him. It ends with Nancy performing her cheer-leader routine as a bump-and-grind burlesque of the most sexually provoc-ative kind. In Nancy's eyes the evening begins with Elliot's insensitive and ill-timed attempt at a brutal seduction just as the couple are leaving for their dinner date. It continues with his flirtation with a voluptuous waitress and ends with his show of self-indulgent jealousy at Nancy's perfectly innocent display of exuberance to her friends.

In another episode the advertising agency started by Michael and Elliot faces ruin. Michael argues, with great responsibility, for the need to see the situation objectively, to accept economic reality, and to file for Chapter 11. Elliot argues, with equally convincing fervor, that he and Michael are too talented to have their business ruined by the loss of one profitable account. He urges improvisation, the securing of more loans, and a greater faith in their combined talents as a perfectly sensible response to the situation.

Neither of these episodes feed viewers the "correct" interpretation of the situation. At different points in each episode the various protagonists, with their antithetical perspectives on the events depicted, are presented as having seen objective reality quite clearly. It is surprising and delightful to realize at the end of these episodes that no single character is blessed with a perfect clarity of perception. These episodes are excellent dramati-zations of the truth that interpretation is all.

Teachers who are trying to encourage their learners to stand outside their habitual frameworks of interpretation and come to a more informed awareness can use such episodes to vivid effect. Discussing the ways in which learners recognize that contradictory views of the same situation can appear convincing and internally consistent to those involved is a very effective exercise. It shows, in a manner that connects dramatically to adults' own experiences, how multiple interpretations can be made of situ-ations that appear to their protagonists to be self-evident.

For anyone teaching the dynamics of intimate relationships, patterns of human communication, conflict resolution, or negotiation, these episodes provide useful case material. In particular they show how self-fulfilling prophecies can operate with devastating effect. Because Nancy expects Elliot to be boorish and brutal, any genuinely affectionate advance he makes is bound to be perceived by her as a clumsy attempt at seduction. Because Elliot expects Michael to be overly cautious in his approach to life,

Michael's prudence and objectivity are bound to be perceived by Elliot as a weak-kneed lack of courage at a crucial moment.

As we watch these episodes, we are subtly drawn into accepting one character's wholly convincing interpretation of a situation—only to find (usually after a commercial break) that we are coming to see the self-evident truth of a completely contradictory point of view held by another character. For commercial television this is an educational and dramatic achievement of a high order. No doubt the show will eventually fall victim to the frustrating contradictory law of television: As soon as an innovative show becomes successful it must be purged of the very originality that ensured its success in the first place. But for now, before it retreats into a simplistic depiction of adult dilemmas, *Thirtysomething* is performing an important educational function in the community.

Developing Media Literacy in the Community

Several techniques can be used in developing media literacy in the community (Brookfield, 1990). One of these is *information mediation analysis*. This technique focuses on the ways in which anchorpersons, news reporters, and chairpersons of discussions function as mediators of information and framers of discourse. Learners can be encouraged to focus on several variables regarding how interviewers mediate discussion: the style the interviewer uses (gladiatorial with "deviant" opinion holders; neutral or deferential with politicians; devil's advocate); the language the interviewer adopts with different interviewees (technical, colloquial, serious, sarcastic, condescending, respectful); whether interviewers rephrase, edit, and interpret for the audience the contributions of guests; and whether the interviewer encourages spontaneous interruptions or controls the flow of discussion.

A second technique is *setting analysis* (Handron, 1988). Here television viewers read the transcript of a broadcast to see how the physical setting of an interview has embedded within it certain messages concerning the symbolic status of the participants. The location and "set" of an interview determine how much credibility the articulation of a certain viewpoint implicitly receives. Viewers can also undertake *question analysis*, in which the questions put to the protagonists in a political event are scrutinized for the preferred meanings embedded in them. They can study whether one side receives strongly critical questioning while the other is allowed a more or less unedited expression of opinion.

Content analysis is a technique familiar to students of popular culture (Masterman, 1980, 1985). Analyzing the content of newspapers, advertisements, and magazines has been a common exercise in school and college settings. The low price of video cassette recorders (VCRs) now means that this technique can be applied in adult learning groups. For example, a media study group could allot responsibility for monitoring a week's news broadcasts on the major networks in order to examine how much time each network devoted to a particular news story. Or a group could focus on a particular issue (for example, a strike or accusations of government corruption) with different learners recording how much prominence various newscasts and current affairs programs gave to the views of different parties involved in the issue. It would also be simple to chart how news stories rose to prominence during various days or weeks and then receded as other items were given attention. Learners in a content analysis group could compare news bulletins on different networks during the breakfast show, at lunchtime, and on the evening news to study changes in tone and content reflecting how one study was treated at different times on the same day.

Viewers might simply clock the amount of time provided for the participants in disputes to air their views. Or they might count the number of questions put to different participants, and reflect on what it means to ask more questions of a particular figure in an event. Another interesting variant on these approaches is *context analysis*. Here learners study whether or not news stories focus on the micro-level—with strong emphasis on the personalities in a dispute—or whether they deal with the macro-level societal or community context within which the issue occurs. They may raise questions about the extent to which news stories give preliminary context-setting explanations of the events and issues they feature. In reporting strikes or demonstrations, for example, do newscasters discuss the causes and history of these events? Or do they simply mention the times, places, and numbers involved before cutting to provocative visual footage of pickets fighting with police, demonstrators burning the flag, and so on?

A final approach to developing media literacy focuses not so much on programs prepared by others as on learners constructing their own programs (Heaney, 1983; Jarvis, 1985). It is a "learning by doing" approach in which the inevitable realities of selection and editing in the construction of TV programs are brought powerfully home. As learners put programs together, they experience how items of information must be left out for reasons of limited time, and they reflect on the decision-making processes that informed their choices about which items were to be included and which rejected. If people have to put together news reports, documentaries, or dramatizations of current events, they experience the same processes experienced in network television.

Conclusion

The mass media are neither smoothly functioning mind manipulators nor courageous critics of the dominant social order. Each media initiative is a psychosocial drama. Understanding the negative influence of mass media in communities, as well as appreciating their power to stimulate critical thought, is important for all educators who seek to explore the full range of learning opportunities and frameworks available in their communities.

References

Berger, A. A. *Media Analysis Techniques.* Newbury Park, Calif.: Sage, 1983.

Brookfield, S. D. "Media Power and the Development of Media Literacy: An Adult Educational Interpretation." *Harvard Educational Review,* 1986, *56* (2), 151–170.

Brookfield, S. D. "Analyzing the Influence of Media on Learners' Perspectives." In J. Mezirow and Associates, *Fostering Critical Reflection in Adulthood: A Guide to Transformative and Emancipatory Learning.* San Francisco: Jossey-Bass, 1990.

Handron, D. "Developing Methods and Techniques for Fostering Media Literacy in Adults." Unpublished doctoral dissertation, Department of Higher and Adult Education, Teachers College, Columbia University, 1988.

Heaney, T. "Materials for Learning and Acting." In J. P. Wilson (ed.), *Materials for Teaching Adults: Selection, Development, and Use.* New Directions for Continuing Education, no. 17. San Francisco: Jossey-Bass, 1983.

Jarvis, P. "Thinking Critically in an Information Society." *Lifelong Learning: An Omnibus of Practice and Research,* 1985, *8* (6), 11–14.

Logan, B. (ed.). *Television Awareness Training.* Nashville, Tenn.: Abingdon, 1979.

Masterman, L. *Teaching About Television.* London: Macmillan, 1980.

Masterman, L. *Teaching the Media.* London: Comedia Publishing Group, 1985.

Stephen D. Brookfield is a professor in the Department of Higher and Adult Education, Teachers College, Columbia University.

Business and industry can make important contributions to building communities of learners, but the main responsibility for using these opportunities still rests with the learner.

Business and Industry for Continuous Learning

Albert K. Wiswell

Business and industry have a special place in contributing to the building of a learning community. It is well documented that the private sector devotes great resources to enhancing work-related learning for employees through the many activities generally considered in the realm of human resource development. Estimates that $210 billion or more is being spent per year on formal and informal employer-provided learning place this activity in the same league as public education, postsecondary education, and higher education (Carnevale, 1986). Less well documented are the contributions made to the community at large by these activities as well as other endeavors in the private sector that contribute to learning.

The spillover of typical training and development activities to the general community of learners takes two general forms. Specific learning experiences for employees and their families intended to enhance performance in the workplace also affect activities away from work. For example, supervisory or management development training often involves interpersonal skills such as negotiation or feedback. If people gain these skills for the purpose of increasing their job effectiveness, nothing precludes them from utilizing them to improve interactions with their family, friends, and acquaintances in the community. Thus, the general community of learners benefits from learning intended to improve job performance.

In addition, employer-initiated activities intended for other reasons such as public relations, corporate image, or marketing can be utilized by citizens who take advantage of it. Business and industry provide learning apart from that intended to enhance the current and future productivity of

employees. Companies are becoming more aware that increased involvement in the community is in their long-term interest. They are realizing
how learning by employees for purposes that do not directly address organizational needs serves the broader organizational mission and how the
general enhancement of those in the community also serves the broader
organizational mission.

The Target Clientele

Most employer-provided learning is obviously directed at the employees of
a particular organization. However, learning for employees is an inherent
part of any learning community. A large part of most people's lives is
devoted to their livelihood, at least in terms of the portion of time they
spend on it. Therefore, the learning that occurs at work is for many people
a significant component of their overall learning experiences. Much of that
learning has the potential for informal dissemination to the community.

Learning for nonemployees is provided by business and industry both
for employees' families as well as the community at large. This can be
through general educational experiences, such as wellness programs, that
can benefit employees and their families. Employee assistance programs
often offer learning opportunities for financial planning, budgeting, and
family issues apart from the counseling services or referrals commonly
considered in this realm. For example, the Marriott Corporation has offered
programs for effective parenting (Skrzycki, 1990) as a response to the need
for dual-wage-earner families to maximize the quality of interactions with
their children.

Special populations such as immigrants, the illiterate, the intellectually
challenged, and minorities are particular targets of the larger role that business
is taking in educating the work force. Partly because of increased demands
for labor and partly because of increased complexity of jobs, employers are
finding themselves in the business of providing English instruction to speakers of other languages and providing basic reading and math skills to the
functionally illiterate. While they usually contract this work to external providers such as community colleges, school systems, or private consultants,
these activities are initiated by and paid for by the employers.

Areas for Learning Opportunities

In actuality, the learning provided through the workplace by business can
take many forms. It ranges in content and purpose from activities intended
to increase current job performance to activities that have only a tangential
relationship to job performance.

Most workplace learning is designed to enhance on-the-job performance. Due to the increased use of technology, this learning often involves

technology that has been recently introduced. The transfer of learning computer applications on a personal computer to areas outside the workplace, for example, is relatively easy to trace. It might increase a person's ability to conduct personal communications, finances, and contributions to community groups. It might also contribute to people's interactions with their children, especially when they are learning similar skills in school. Learning these technical skills might also result in improved general thinking skills. Transfer of learning outside the workplace is more difficult to envisage for such technical skills as operating a machine designed for a particular function. But even this learning could have an effect on a worker's life beyond the job.

Career development is gaining an increasing role in the overall human resource development programs of many companies. These efforts are generally focused on assisting employees to plan their careers, gain further education, and learn about opportunities in the organization for attaining their career goals. From the organization's perspective, these programs serve two purposes: developing employees within the organization and reducing turnover (Gilley and Eggland, 1989). From the perspective of employees, career development means maximizing their potential to develop their capabilities. This learning benefits not only the employees and their families but ultimately society in general, as people are empowered to make their maximum contributions—with the accompanying rewards.

Enhancing Quality of Life Through Learning

Many learning opportunities provided by employers are considered as additional benefits, at least from the employer's viewpoint. Other learning opportunities are regarded as improving the general well-being of the employee but may not directly contribute to job-related issues. Some companies, for example, reimburse tuition for any bona fide education, regardless of its relevance to the employee's current job.

These learning experiences can enhance avocational skills that have no direct relevance to the job. The supervisor of janitorial services who takes company-sponsored courses at the community college in computer programming does so because of an interest in personal home computing. This person may never be in a job that requires programming skills, even if he or she moves into an upper-level managerial role. This learning experience, however, may not only result in a more adaptable and savvy employee but may also increase commitment to the organization because of the reimbursement.

Wellness programs are an integral part of many corporate human resource development programs. They typically involve a variety of learning activities such as nutrition education, exercise, and development of healthy habits including cessation of smoking and reduction of alcohol consumption. This is important for the organization because healthier employees have less absenteeism and fewer medical claims. These areas of learning also contribute to family health and increase community awareness of these issues.

Leisure activity can also be enhanced through company-sponsored activities. Sports are one form of this involvement. Sponsoring teams for softball or bowling, for example, helps to involve employees in these activities. The sponsorship may also extend to teams whose members are not employees but customers or children. Apart from the learning directly related to improving one's skill in the sport, these activities also afford employees opportunities for demonstrating leadership and organizational skills.

The last area of company-sponsored learning may have no direct effect other than fostering a zest for lifelong learning as described by Houle (1984). Learning for the sake of learning may be the most important contributor to building a community of learners who value inquiry and interaction. Learning can be contagious. It can lead people to learn all sorts of activities that could permeate every aspect of their lives.

Educational Partnerships for the Entire Learning Community

Partnerships are a growing part of business involvement in the community. In these arrangements, organizations enter into agreements with schools, libraries, or other agencies to provide resources for learning. This effort can take the form of providing guest speakers, offering long-term assistance in educational programs (such as tutoring), or providing equipment or finances that improve the agency's ability to offer learning opportunities.

IBM is one of many corporations that has involved itself in the partnership arena in a variety of ways across the country. IBM has donated scientific equipment (not limited to computers) for use in classrooms through adopt-a-school relationships and other arrangements with elementary and secondary schools. The company has also worked with retiring employees and other IBM workers who wish a transition to teaching by sponsoring them in teaching certification programs at universities.

Sales percentage contributions by grocery chains and drug stores are a recent innovation that provides direct financial support to schools and other nonprofit agencies. In these programs, customers save their sales receipts and turn them in to the participating agencies. A percentage of gross receipts is then returned to the agency by the corporation—either directly in cash or in the form of computer equipment.

From a business viewpoint, partnerships serve primarily a public relations purpose and a long-term recruitment strategy for future employees. There are other beneficial outcomes, however, including increased learning for all students or contributions to the learning community in general.

Business partnerships with education will surely continue to grow in significance in the coming years.

Learning Centers for the Populace

Learning centers may be devoted solely to employee and consumer learning, or businesses may engage in them as part of their overall operation. Many building supply stores, for example, may offer Saturday morning lessons in deck building or landscaping, hoping to encourage sales of the materials they sell. Sewing centers may be specifically oriented to providing learning. It is commonplace to offer free, unlimited instruction in operating sewing machines—especially the high-tech computerized machines on today's market that approach the complexity of the personal computer. Stretch and Sew is a franchised instructional network aimed at assisting people to utilize many of today's easy-care knit products and the machines designed to work with them.

A few years ago, Texas Instruments (TI) established a network of learning centers across the country for the purpose of teaching various computer skills to the public. They taught courses ranging from basic computer literacy and word processing to advanced programming and graphics. All were designed to encourage use of TI home computers, but they were offered at a reasonable cost with a high degree of transferability to other systems. These centers enjoyed considerable success and were ended only because of changes in the product line.

Incidental Contributions by Business

A number of corporate activities lead to learning as an incidental by-product of the activity, not as a intentional goal. Though incidental, they are surely not insignificant. These activities may be as formalized as the support of a company museum or as intangible as the way they decorate the lobbies of their buildings or promote their products and services.

Corporate museums are more than public relations. This may be the main intent of the companies that create such institutions, but their contribution to the learning community is inestimable. The Corning Glass Works, for example, maintains a museum in Corning, New York, that is virtually a history of civilization from prehistoric times to the present with respect to the use and development of glass and glass products. It is not only an educational experience offered to the public but also a major tourist attraction for upper New York state.

Trade shows can be used for education as well as commerce. A wide range of industries use exhibitions and trade shows as vehicles for presenting new products and technology to consumers as well as retailers for the industry. Auto shows, boat shows, and computer shows are some of the more popular variants of this potential learning experience. Conventions and trade shows are big business in themselves, but the learning opportunities they present are often well worth the effort of attendance.

Lobbies and halls of office buildings can be interesting sources of learning because of displays constructed to educate customers, employees, and visitors. Often companies display products and illustrations of their manufacturing process. The Motorola plant in Austin, Texas, is an interesting example. The site for manufacturing some of the most advanced computer chips in the industry, Motorola has created displays of the process of converting a slab of silicon rock through the stages of processing that result in hundreds of sophisticated memory chips. The plant has also presented animated displays illustrating the low power requirements of these chips. Prototype computers powered by a live mouse running in an exercise wheel or by a lime connected to the circuitry by two small wires invite anyone willing to stop and look to participate in this interesting learning experience.

Many companies purchase and commission works of art for display in their buildings for the pleasure of employees and customers. These works are usually accessible to the public and represent a great cultural learning opportunity. The Westfields Conference Center is a for-profit enterprise adjacent to the Dulles International Airport outside of Washington, D.C., that makes its foyers and hallways sources of learning by decorating them with eighteenth-century artwork, period furniture, and commissioned sculpture and chandeliers. They even provide visitors with a twenty-page booklet describing and documenting the works of art. Workshop and retreat participants as well as restaurant customers may browse through the halls and learn about the artifacts as they proceed to their business or dinner engagements.

Advertisements may be the last refuge for the scoundrels of commerce, but often they are also the last refuge of learning. Actually, advertisements can be used effectively as learning experiences. Most advertising copy could probably not be considered material for learning—but some can, especially if consumers with a skeptical perspective use them as such. An intriguing example of advertising that fits this category is a brochure and floppy disk for personal computers distributed by the Buick Division of General Motors (General Motors Corporation, 1989). The computer disk presents technical descriptions, pricing tables, and comparison charts for all its current models—interesting information for persons contemplating an automobile purchase. But it also includes an interactive road atlas identifying the interstate system, major cities and state capitals, national parks, and other attractions. Additionally, distances between points can be found and a game is included that challenges players to identify their location when shown a small isolated segment of the map.

Expanding the Learning Community

Witting and unwitting contributions to the learning community by business and industry have great potential as a major social force. Obviously, not all these contributions to the learning community are intentionally designed as such by the businesses that provide them. The intent may be public relations, marketing, or even other enterprises in addition to efforts to improve worker productivity. Making use of them for learning is ultimately the responsibility of the learner. Perhaps this is the key to describing a community of learners: Individuals take responsibility for learning—for themselves and for their fellow learners.

A learning community is characterized by people who are sensitized to observing their environment, its effect on them, and their effect on it. They develop notions about these observations and are disposed to share these ideas with others in seeking their reactions. They also hold the expectation that others will share observations and notions of their experience. Using opportunities for learning—compliments of business and industry—can play a major role in this process. Contributing to the learning community is good business for business, but the populace can gain many opportunities for learning by taking advantage of these contributions.

References

Carnevale, A. "The Learning Enterprise." *Training and Development Journal,* 1986, *40* (1), 18–26.

General Motors Corporation. *Buick Dimensions 1990.* Flint, Mich.: Buick Dimensions Distribution Center, 1989.

Gilley, J., and Eggland, S. *Principles of Human Resource Development.* Reading, Mass.: Addison-Wesley, 1989.

Houle, C. *Patterns of Learning.* San Francisco: Jossey-Bass, 1984.

Skrzycki, C. "Marriott Steps in to Help Employees Raise Families." *Washington Post,* February 2, 1990, pp. a1, a8.

Albert K. Wiswell is assistant professor of human resource development at the Virginia Polytechnic Institute and State University, Northern Virginia Graduate Center, Falls Church, Virginia.

For over seventy-five years the Cooperative Extension Service has served American communities through formal, nonformal, and informal educational programs.

Cooperative Extension as Community Education Developer

David W. Price

Heralded as the single largest adult education agency in the world and widely known to rural Americans as the "County Extension," the Cooperative Extension Service has for more than seventy-five years developed communities of learners through formal, nonformal, and informal educational programs. The local community has been the locus of Extension Service program operations since its establishment by congressional mandate in 1914. The Smith-Lever Act of that year provided for a national adult education system linking the resources of land-grant colleges with the needs and aspirations of people throughout local communities.

As originally conceived, county-based extension agents, or "itinerant teachers" as they were called, were to "aid in diffusing among the people of the United States useful and practical information on subjects relating to agriculture and home economics" (U.S. Stat. at Large, Vol. 38, p. 372). Not only has "subjects relating to" always been broadly interpreted to include a variety of topics highly relevant to people's lives, but several amendments to the original legislation have further broadened Extension Service programs. Extension Service efforts include projects in agriculture and natural resources, youth development and family living, community and rural development, and continuing professional education. With few exceptions, the Cooperative Extension Service maintains at least one full-time professional Extension educator in each of the 3,150 counties in the United States (Rasmussen, 1989). Throughout its history, the thrust of Extension Service programming has consistently remained practical and highly relevant to local communities.

This chapter examines the Extension Service's role in community education. It addresses the scope of Extension Service work in terms of community-based lifelong education, profiles its approaches to program development and delivery, and concludes with a discussion concerning the future of the Extension Service as community education developer.

Extension Services as Lifelong Education

The diversity of subjects and learners served by Extension programs may be usefully addressed in terms of lifelong education. As described by Galbraith and Sundet (in press), lifelong education is vertically integrated (covering the lifespan from birth to death), horizontally integrated (linking learning and life), and emphasizes learning to learn—a policy that strengthens people's desire and capacity to learn continually from their environment. Moreover, the local community serves as the "fundamental locus of lifelong educational practice" (Galbraith and Price, in press). Few educational organizations reflect these ideals and practices more closely than does the Extension Service. Lifelong education, then, offers a particularly relevant framework by which Extension Service programs can be described.

Vertical Integration. Extension educational efforts include parenting programs focused on early childhood development, youth education through the Extension's nationwide 4-H Club program, and related developmental activities for youth and teens. In addition, a variety of educational opportunities are provided to adults of all ages. In recent years, Extension Service programs have targeted senior adults, including the active retired, as well as addressing the learning needs of the frail elderly and their caregivers. Although most Extension Service programs address young and middle adult audiences, the Extension's willingness and ability to respond to the educational needs of people of all ages attests to its commitment to vertically integrated education.

Horizontal Integration. The original legislative mandate for useful and practical education virtually assured an Extension system uniquely concerned with the everyday learning needs of people, as well as in the family, leisure, social, occupational, and professional aspects of their lives. In submitting the bill to Congress, the House Committee on Agriculture envisioned a system of county-based Extension agents that were "to assume leadership in every movement, whatever it may be, the aim of which is better farming, better living, more happiness, more education, and better citizenship" (U.S. Congress, 1913, p. 5). The Extension Service has historically been highly integrated with the lives of individuals and their communities, characterized by county-based programs concerned with enhancing the quality of life.

This holistic, micro-level educational approach has fostered a diversity of relevant programs: educational efforts aimed at helping farmers increase production and efficiency, assisting small business operators with marketing and sound business practices, and nutrition education for the community at large as well as programs targeting low-income community members. Additionally, the Extension Service provides continuing professional development programs for teachers, nurses, lawyers, and various other occupational groups, develops community schools whereby community members share special skills and talents, and organizes community-wide economic development and other improvement projects. The Extension Service is also widely known for its publication and dissemination of educational bulletins that offer practical advice on a multitude of topics highly relevant to people's lives.

Although these educational efforts exemplify Extension Services nationally, not every county Extension program includes the variety in educational effort mentioned. Several factors, including the cooperative funding mix (local, state, and federal) of Extension Services and the reliance on county-specific program priorities, result in somewhat uneven Extension programming nationwide. Still, the capacity and willingness of Extension Services to provide useful and practical educational programs relating to individual and community life attests to its strong orientation to the horizontal integration of community lifelong education.

Learning to Learn. The concept of learning to learn lies at the heart of Extension Service educational philosophy—which stresses teaching people how to think rather than what to think—and views education as "basic in stimulating individual initiative, self-determination, and leadership" (Prawl, Medlin, and Gross, 1984, pp. 30–31). The Extension educator functions as a catalyst in the educational process. Although highly competent in a specific discipline—agriculture or business management, for example—the Extension educator focuses on the facilitation of learning rather than merely the transmission of content.

Program Development and Delivery

As a partnership among the federal government, state land-grant universities, and local counties, the development and delivery of Extension Service programs becomes a complex process in which each partner is involved at various points and to varying degrees. For the most part, federal and state roles are limited to the determination of broad program priorities of national and statewide concern, orchestration of state plans of work (based largely on locally developed plans), and the determination of staffing patterns and program funding mechanisms. It is primarily at the local community level that detailed plans for Extension educational programs are determined and educational experiences ultimately provided. This discussion, then, concerns the development and delivery of educational programs by county-based Extension Service educators.

Developing Extension Programs. Program development in the Extension Service has evolved through various phases in its history. Early Extension work was characterized by educational initiatives predetermined at federal and state levels. County Extension workers soon recognized, however, the limitations of externally driven planning. Successful Extension programs, they found, were developed *with* people rather than for people, and a highly participatory grass-roots approach to Extension Services program development emerged. Program development was further modified with the trend-based programming phase, in which program decisions were based on extensive fact gathering and the analysis of socioeconomic trends. This approach continued to involve learners in educational planning, but special-interest and commodity groups came to constitute the participatory dimension. This shift had the effect of fragmenting the community-wide emphasis of the grass-roots approach and laid the foundation for what is currently termed "disciplinary programming" (Dalgaard and others, 1988).

Modern program development in the Extension Service incorporates major components from each of the three approaches. The original predetermined approach enables the Extension Service to respond quickly and directly to major programs of national concern. Examples include the Expanded Food and Nutrition Education Program (EFNEP), which targeted low-income families for nutrition education, and a host of special projects in response to the family farm crisis of the 1980s. Most Extension programs, however, are developed at the county level through a combination of the grass-roots and trend-based approaches. Although no single program model is applied by Extension Services nationally, the process typically involves certain major components.

First a situation analysis is conducted to identify community needs and the affected clientele. Relevant environmental factors are considered, and a rationale for Extension Service involvement is articulated. Program objectives describe the end results anticipated from Extension intervention. An educational plan of action addresses planned learning experiences and activities, including educational methods to be used, activity locations, and schedule. Program resources (financial and human) necessary to carry out the program are determined, and plans are made for securing resources not readily available within the organization. Finally, a plan is developed for evaluating program outcomes and reporting results to constituencies.

Although Extension program development is presented here as a linear process, in practice it is continuous and cyclical. Adjustments in the program plan may frequently be made, and program operations in one sphere often lead to the recognition of community problems and learning needs in other spheres, further programming, and so on. The development of Extension programs is carried forward in the community context and in concert with local people. Involvement techniques, especially crucial in the needs assessment phase of the process, include community surveys, interviews with key informants, Delphi studies, neighborhood and community forums, participant observation, and the extensive use of county Extension program planning committees comprised of local volunteers. By using a variety of involvement techniques that facilitate the active participation of community members, not only do Extension educators ensure highly relevant educational programs but the process of program development itself becomes a meaningful learning experience for the people involved.

Fundamental shifts in Extension Service program development have recently appeared in response to a number of pressures, including fiscal austerity and increasing demands for public accountability (Forest, 1989). Two separate national committees, the National Initiatives Coordinating Committee and the Extension Service Futures Task Force, have called for a move toward issue-based programming, and the Extension Service is now embarked on a course of organizational renewal that suggests major changes in future programming and staffing patterns (Dalgaard and others, 1988). Issue programming emphasizes interdisciplinary team approaches to issues of wide public concern identified at county, state, and national levels, a renewed attention to community-wide program development, and proactive rather than reactive educational initiatives by Extension educators.

In northwestern Missouri, for example, an interdisciplinary team of Extension educators recently organized to address regional concerns for water quality. Specifically, the project involves Extension professionals in community development, environmental design, agricultural engineering, and youth education who will function as a team to orchestrate extensive community involvement in a variety of educational activities relating to the pollution of area groundwater (Orton, 1990). Distinctive features of the project, indicative of issue programming, include the integration of educational initiatives by several disciplinary specialists to address many facets of a complex public issue—in this case, water pollution.

It will take several years to fully implement the charges indicated by the issue programming movement, and it remains to be seen to what extent the changes will reshape the organization and affect learners in local communities. It is apparent, however, that issue-based programming constitutes the latest phase in the continuing evolution of Extension Service approaches to program development.

Delivering Programs. Extension educational methods include formal, nonformal, and informal approaches to facilitating learning in the community. These categories, while a useful classification scheme, are not mutually exclusive and are strongly interrelated. Effective Extension programs include the complementary use of methods from each of the categories.

Formal educational methods involve individual and group program delivery and usually require advance registration and the payment of fees by participants. They often involve some type of certification or credentialing and the assignment of continuing education units (CEUs) or academic credit. Because of the credentialing aspects, formal programs are often taught and administered by Extension Service educators in cooperation with other organizations such as professional societies, state agencies, and academic divisions of higher education institutions. Formal program delivery methods include conferences consisting of a series of lectures and workshops addressing a general topic and involving large numbers of participants; institutes made up of several short instructional meetings or workshops and organized around some specialized topic for a specific group of learners; short courses involving a series of brief class meetings over an extended period of time and addressing a specialized topic; and academic courses that consist of a series of class meetings over an extended period of time or individualized study coupled with correspondence, videotaped, or other remote-delivered lessons on a special topic. Formal program delivery methods provide learners in a community with opportunities for personal and professional growth while meeting their needs for formal recognition of learning for various certifications and licenses.

Nonformal educational methods make up the greater portion of the Extension educator's methodological repertoire and enable the Extension Service to facilitate learning in a variety of community settings. Space limitations preclude a full discussion of all the nonformal learning techniques applied by the Extension educator, but some of the more prevalent ones are addressed here.

The demonstration method dates back to the very beginnings of Extension Service work and is still in popular use today (Forest, 1989). Agricultural demonstration relies on a system of community "cooperators" who volunteer portions of their land for the application of particular farming practices under the supervision of an Extension educator. Periodic "field days" are held at the demonstration site in which other area farmers are invited to see firsthand the application and results of the new techniques. Similarly, Extension educators use the demonstration method to teach home energy conservation techniques, business management practices, and an endless variety of other practical arts and skills.

The community forum is widely used by Extension educators to facilitate awareness and learning on issues of community-wide concern. Presentations on a given issue by recognized experts are followed with in-depth discussion and issue analysis by forum participants. Forum presenters may be local community leaders, outside resource people, or Extension educators themselves. The Extension educator often uses the nominal technique or other group methods to encourage discussion and facilitate consensus when appropriate.

Training and visitation (T&V) is an oft-used Extension method whereby learners participate in periodic group instruction at a central location, supplemented by individual consultation with the educator at participants' homes, farms, or places of business. Specialized agricultural practices for farmers, parenting and family dynamics for families, small-business management for new business owners, organizational development for community agency executives, local government operations for public officials—all are appropriate T&V subjects. Apart from the T&V approach, individual consultation with learners in person, by telephone, and by mail (including electronic mail) constitutes a frequently used and highly effective nonformal educational method.

Seminars and workshops are usually conducted in small groups and address specialized topics relevant to particular occupations or professions. Seminars emphasize discussion and sharing of expertise by participants themselves, whereas workshops emphasize hands-on skill development and guided practice led by the Extension educator.

Educational field trips and tours take groups of learners to sites of interest for direct observation and study, followed by critical analysis and discussion led by the Extension educator. Field trips and tours may take farmers to innovative farm operations, community leaders to unique community improvement projects in neighboring cities, and interested citizens to new local industries or offices of local government. Generally a field trip involves a single site visit of a few hours, whereas a tour involves several sites over an extended period.

Informal educational methods are those that enable community members to develop new attitudes, awareness, and knowledge through experiences in natural social settings and in the course of their day-to-day lives (Brookfield, 1983; Roberts, 1979). Radio and television spots and regular educational columns in local newspapers enable Extension educators to reach wide audiences of learners on a variety of topics. Educational newsletters, public exhibits, and the distribution of bulletins and flyers on a variety of educational topics are additional methods that further informal learning in the community. Community action projects orchestrated and assisted by Extension educators also provide innumerable opportunities for involved citizens to learn informally as they study their community and work together to attain common objectives and resolve community problems.

Extension Service educators employ a wide range of methods in the delivery of community educational programs. Rarely is any one method used alone. Extension educators normally mix and phase several formal, nonformal, and informal educational methods in order to attain specified program objectives. Moreover, Extension educators do not operate in isolation from the many local organizations, agencies, and institutions. Programs are often carried forward in close collaboration with various community-based institutions with educative potential in order to bring a wide range of community resources to bear on learning needs and community problems. It is through such broad interagency approaches and a diverse educational methodology that the Extension Service contributes toward developing and sustaining community education infrastructures and builds communities of learners.

Future Prospects

The Cooperative Extension Service founded its reputation on useful educational service to local communities, and very early in its history it embraced the participatory approach to developing and delivering community educational programs. Although the Extension Service has undergone a number of changes in its history, as American society itself has changed, the organization has maintained and even enhanced its commitment to community relevance and public involvement. Extension has demonstrated its capacity for structural change while preserving organizational values that, when translated into educational practice, provide meaningful learning and development for individuals and communities. Its continued success as a prominent feature of the American educational landscape will depend on this capacity for change—not so much for a periodic realignment, as has been its experience to date, but for continuous adjustment to the rapidly changing social, economic, and political realities affecting American communities. The current Extension Service emphasis on issue-based programming— calling for proactive interdisciplinary team approaches to complex human problems and for more fluid and less permanent staffing patterns—reflects this dynamic change. It suggests an organizational will to adjust its structure to an era of rapid change.

Current trends affecting Extension programming in the community include new telecommunications technologies, the continuing public accountability movement, and demographic shifts. New telecommunications technologies are opening many opportunities for Extension Service program delivery. Computer-mediated teaching and electronic mail, dial-access audio, interactive video, and a host of electronic technologies yet to be developed will quickly become standard media for Extension education work—both for individual consultation and for group teaching.

Demands for accountability to lawmakers and the general public will continue to influence program development and delivery in the future (Forest, 1989), discouraging innovation and bold program initiatives at a time when they are most needed to address increasingly complex community problems. Constant scrutiny of program plans and the Extension professional's time tend to result in conservative programming, conveniently measured objectives, and evaluations designed more for documentation than for program improvement.

Demographic changes suggest the culture is giving way to a more mature, better educated, and more sophisticated society (Forest, 1989; Galbraith and Price, in press). Learners exhibit greater independence and are more demanding consumers in the educational marketplace for methods, formats, content, and levels suited to their unique characteristics and needs. While remaining flexible and sensitive to this changing environment itself, the Extension Service is in a unique position to provide leadership in responding community-wide to diverse educational needs.

The Extension Service has a long and successful history of educational service to American communities. Present and future social, economic, and technological trends will continue to challenge Extension educators to provide timely and meaningful educational experiences relating to the many facets of individual and community life and to an increasingly diverse population of community lifelong learners.

References

Brookfield, S. D. *Adult Learners, Adult Education and the Community*. New York: Teachers College Press, 1983.

Dalgaard, K. A., Brazzel, M., Liles, R. T., Sanderson, D., and Taylor-Powell, E. *Issues Programming in Extension*. St. Paul: Minnesota Extension Service, 1988.

Forest, L. B. "The Cooperative Extension Service." In S. B. Merriam and P. M. Cunningham (eds.), *Handbook of Adult and Continuing Education*. San Francisco: Jossey-Bass, 1989.

Galbraith, M. W., and Price, D. W. "Community Adult Education." In M. W. Galbraith and P. A. Sundet (eds.), *Education in the Rural American Community: A Lifelong Process*. Malabar, Fla.: Krieger, in press.

Galbraith, M. W., and Sundet, P. A. "Lifelong Education and Community." In M. W. Galbraith and P. A. Sundet (eds.), *Education in the Rural American Community: A Lifelong Process*. Malabar, Fla.: Krieger, in press.

Orton, H. "Water Quality Public Awareness and Education Project." Northwest Missouri Extension Region Water Quality Committee, University Extension, St. Joseph, Missouri. April 1990. Photocopy.

Phifer, B., List, F., and Faulkner, B. "History of Community Development in America." In J. A. Christenson and J. W. Robinson (eds.), *Community Development in America*. Ames: Iowa State University Press, 1980.

Prawl, W., Medlin, R., and Gross, J. *Adult and Continuing Education Through the Cooperative Extension Service*. Columbia: Extension Division, University of Missouri–Columbia, 1984.

Rasmussen, W. D. *Taking the University to the People: Seventy-Five Years of Cooperative Extension*. Ames: Iowa State University Press, 1989.

Roberts, H. *Community Development: Learning and Action*. Toronto: University of Toronto Press, 1979.

U.S. Congress. House Committee on Agriculture. *Cooperative Agricultural Extension Work*. 63rd Cong. 2d sess. H. Rept. 110. Serial 6558. 1913.

David W. Price has been a community development specialist with the Cooperative Extension Service in Missouri and a program development and evaluation specialist with the National Geographic Society's Missouri Geography Education Program. He is currently a Ph.D. candidate in higher and adult education at the University of Missouri–Columbia.

The foregoing chapters detailing the educational opportunities for adults provided by community organizations can be usefully examined from the perspective of choice.

Building Communities of Learners

Michael W. Galbraith

Social, demographic, technological, and economic forces contribute to the changing nature of community as well as the inherent need for its members to maintain the skill and motivation to pursue a variety of learning interests throughout their lives. This requires communities of learners who are thoughtful and autonomous and know how to use multiple resources in the community. A learning community calls for discriminating consumers of educational services and learning opportunities. The previous chapters contain a rich diversity of thought as it pertains to educational consumer and educational provider. At the heart of community education is the notion that building a community of learners requires choices. These choices are made by adult learners, community organizations, and educators of adults.

Adult Learners' Choices

In Chapter One, I suggest that the concept of community can be viewed from various perspectives such as location, interest, and function, as well as demographic and psychographic dimensions. Adult learners may be members of several communities, each contributing to a different dimension that fulfills some specific, culturally constructed, and contextual need in their lives, whether personal, professional, social, spiritual, or recreational. Choices are then made by adult learners when it comes to what, why, where, and how learning will occur. Will these choices maintain what Peshkin (1982) calls community integrity—that is, will they allow for a sense of unity and wholeness shared by members of that community? How will these choices affect individualism, self-reliance, and moral, social, and political discourse—as well as relationships that are connected to the work, religious, and family community? Certainly a reflection on the ethical dimensions of choices made by adult learners seems warranted.

Adult learners make other choices when it comes to educational opportunities provided by community organizations. Most choices are voluntary. However, a distinction must be made between the learner within a community organization and the learner who voluntarily seeks education offered by a community organization. Adults who work within community organizations may be mandated to engage in certain educational and training activities. For example, Victoria Marsick's chapter on human service organizations (Chapter Six) suggests that certain agencies provide educational opportunities that help staff personnel to reach the agency's goals. Some of this training may be mandatory. Albert Wiswell, in his discussion of business and industry in Chapter Nine, stresses that some work-related learning may be mandated while other learning opportunities are voluntary. Personnel in some of the other community organizations, such as libraries, churches, museums, social and fraternal organizations, and the Cooperative Extension Service, may be confronted with the same situation in which learning choices are not voluntary.

If adult learners seek educational opportunities provided by community organizations, however, then various choices are made. One of the first choices is to decide whether or not a need exists. This is followed by determining the purpose of wanting to learn something new. What is the interest level? How will it contribute to fulfilling the identified need, whether for social, personal, political, economic, intellectual, or recreational purposes? Can a community organization be found that will assist in fulfilling the learning purpose? Is the learning opportunity available through public or private organizations? Can I participate as a member of the community at large? What learning methods are used? Will independence in approaching this learning be welcomed? All of these questions, as well as others, require choices to be made by the adult learner. Participation or nonparticipation will be determined by learners' decisions in relation to the community organization in which they seek educational opportunities.

Community Organizations' Choices

The community organizations described in the preceding chapters have made numerous choices relating to how they utilize education to meet their varied missions. They too must begin with philosophical choices concerning their provision of education. The foremost question that must be addressed relates to the issue of why provide education? Is it really a component of the mission, or is the rationale based on a market-driven mentality? It is evident from the foregoing chapters that an explicit connection is made between mission and providing educational opportunities to adult learners. This can be seen in Chapter Two by Trenton Ferro, for example, who points out that most social and fraternal organizations mention the importance of education in their mission statements. Not only do these organizations inform, educate, and support their members but they also inform, educate, and support people in the public sector through various activities. Similar purposes can be seen in the other chapters as well that address libraries (Chapter Three), religious institutions (Chapter Four), community education for older adults (Chapter Five), human service organizations (Chapter Six), museums (Chapter Seven), the mass media (Chapter Eight), business and industry (Chapter Nine), and Cooperative Extension (Chapter Ten). Though different in their respective purposes and approaches, each sector has recognized an educational mission as part of its purpose.

Other choices are made by community organizations, as well, that relate to educational opportunities: Who should they serve? Should they target educational programs to diverse populations such as women, minorities, or the disadvantaged? How often should they be offered? Who in the organization should decide what programs will be offered? How will these programs be supported? Should they be cost-effective? Should learners be charged a fee for participating—and if so on what basis should fees be established? Are organizational staff able to assist in helping adults learn? Should programs be organized on the premise that adults are independent and self-directed learners?

Community organizations have been quite successful in using education as an allied function of their overall purpose. They assist community members in pursuing various learning needs, whether for personal, social, recreational, professional, or intellectual reasons. Given this provision of educational opportunity, the specific organization must make choices grounded in ethical behavior and sound decision making.

Educators' Choices

Griffith (1989) differentiates between an adult educator and an educator of adults by suggesting that educators of adults "have focused goals that typically address pressing problems in a single sector [and] have practical concerns and . . . typically address single programmatic issues through education" (pp. 5-6). This statement captures the essence of those educators of adults who work in community organizations. In addressing programmatic issues, educators of adults must make choices concerning the teaching and learning encounter with adult learners. Just like adult learners and community organizations, educators of adults must do an "ethics check" as well as determine whether their instructional approaches, activities, and programs are grounded in solid adult learning procedures and principles.

Is there, for example, an understanding of how adults learn and how their shifting needs influence the teaching and learning encounter? What educational philosophy does the educator practice? How do philosophy and teaching style influence instructional methods? Should adult learners be helped to become more reflective and critical? While this list is not exhaustive, it does suggest that educators of adults have important choices to make if the educational encounter is going to be rewarding for those engaged in community-based education.

Conclusion

Community is the foundation of a free and democratic society. Building communities of independent, thoughtful, and autonomous learners is one way to sustain the democratic process. Community organizations have contributed to this process by offering diverse educational opportunities to adult learners. While each community exhibits a host of educational opportunities, the learning itself does not belong to the community as a group but to the individual member of the community. Through this process, individuals find satisfaction through context-specific, value-laden, and socially constructed learning experiences. Through community organizations, individuals contribute to the community at large by gaining a better understanding of themselves, by finding meaning in work, family, religion, and community, by contributing something to the public welfare, and by providing a different voice in a common tradition. Education through community organizations contributes to the good community that is anchored in individualism and opportunity for free choice.

References

Griffith, W. S. "Has Adult and Continuing Education Fulfilled Its Early Promise?" In B. A. Quigley (ed.), *Fulfilling the Promise of Adult and Continuing Education*. New Directions for Continuing Education, no. 44. San Francisco: Jossey-Bass, 1989.
Peshkin, A. *The Imperfect Union*. Chicago: University of Chicago Press, 1982.

Michael W. Galbraith is associate professor of adult education and coordinator of graduate studies in adult education at Temple University, Philadelphia.

INDEX

ORDERING INFORMATION

NEW DIRECTIONS FOR ADULT AND CONTINUING EDUCATION is a series of paperback books that explores issues of common interest to instructors, administrators, counselors, and policy makers in a broad range of adult and continuing education settings—such as colleges and universities, extension programs, businesses, the military, prisons, libraries, and museums. Books in the series are published quarterly in Fall, Winter, Spring, and Summer and are available for purchase by subscription as well as by single copy.

SUBSCRIPTIONS for 1990 cost $42.00 for individuals (a savings of 20 percent over single-copy prices) and $56.00 for institutions, agencies, and libraries. Please do not send institutional checks for personal subscriptions. Standing orders are accepted.

SINGLE COPIES cost $12.95 when payment accompanies order. (California, New Jersey, New York, and Washington, D.C., residents please include appropriate sales tax.) Billed orders will be charged postage and handling.

DISCOUNTS FOR QUANTITY ORDERS are available. Please write to the address below for information.

ALL ORDERS must include either the name of an individual or an official purchase order number. Please submit your order as follows:
Subscriptions: specify series and year subscription is to begin
Single copies: include individual title code (such as CE1)

MAIL ALL ORDERS TO:
Jossey-Bass Inc., Publishers
350 Sansome Street
San Francisco, California 94104

FOR SALES OUTSIDE OF THE UNITED STATES CONTACT:
Maxwell Macmillan International Publishing Group
866 Third Avenue
New York, New York 10022